Another collection of classic columns from Neil Haverson

Fortress H:

The Aubergine Bake Repeats

Eastern Daily Press

Published by Eastern Counties Newspapers, Prospect House,
Rouen Road, Norwich, Norfolk, NR1 1RE.

Printed and bound by Page Bros, Mile Cross Lane, Norwich.

ISBN 0-9502952-8-0

Produced by Peter Waters.

Photography by Bill Smith.

To Mrs H

Who stops me from getting bored

Contents

THE AUBERGINE BAKE – by Mrs H

I am surprised that the Aubergine Bake has captured the imagination of so many readers. But let me set the record straight on one or two points.

The way Neil goes on about it you'd think I serve this meal up every week but we don't have it anywhere near as often as he would have you believe! Besides, there's no way I could get Brats Major and Minor to eat it regularly.

In fact, I don't know of a dish called Aubergine Bake. The two meals I usually make are Cashew Nut Moussaka and Aubergine Parmesan.

Both these recipes are supposed to serve 4 but if you are feeding gannets like those at Fortress H, they'll probably only stretch to 3 portions.

CASHEW NUT MOUSSAKA

Preparation time 50 mins. Cooking time 40 mins

Ingredients
1 large aubergine thinly sliced
2 tsp (10ml) olive oil
1 onion chopped
1 clove garlic, crushed
4 oz (125g) mushrooms, sliced
1 green pepper, deseeded and sliced
2 oz (50g) unsalted cashew nuts, roughly chopped if large
1 oz (25g) wholemeal breadcrumbs
1 tbsp (15ml) tomato puree
2 tsp (10ml) chopped fresh basil
1tbsp (15ml) shoyu
1/4 pint (150ml) water
1 oz (25g) wholemeal flour
1/2 pint (300ml) skimmed milk
1 egg
2 oz (50g) Cheddar cheese grated
salt and black pepper
2 tsp (10ml) grated parmesan cheese

Method

1. Put the aubergine slices on to a large baking tray which has been lightly brushed with 1/2 teaspoon of the oil. Brush the tops of the aubergine slices with another 1/2 teaspoon of oil. Bake in a preheated oven at Gas Mark 5, 375°F, 190°C for 10 minutes then remove from the oven.

2. Heat the remaining oil in a large frying pan and gently fry the onion and garlic for 4-5 minutes. Add the mushrooms and pepper, cover and cook gently for a further 10 minutes.

3. Stir in the cashew nuts, breadcrumbs, tomato puree, basil, shoyu and sufficient water to make a moist mixture. Check the seasoning. you can use soy sauce in place of shoyu but the flavour is not so strong.

4. Put about 1/2 the onion and nut mixture into the base of a large casserole or ovenproof dish. Top with half of the aubergine slices. Then put the remaining onion mixture and cover with the rest of the aubergine slices.

5. Mix the flour, milk and egg in a blender or food processor until smooth. Alternatively, put the flour into a large bowl, beat the egg with the milk, then gradually beat into the flour.

6. Put the milk mixture into a small pan and slowly bring to the boil, stirring continuously. Simmer for 3-4 minutes until thickened , stirring continuously. Remove from the heat and stir in the cheese. Check the seasoning.

7. Pour the cheese sauce over the aubergine mixture. Sprinkle with Parmesan cheese. Cover the dish.

8. Bake in the oven for 35-40 minutes, uncovered for the last 10 minutes and garnish with tomato segments. I usually serve it with a side salad.

AUBERGINE PARMESAN

Ingredients
1 lb (450g) potatoes
1 lb 9450g) aubergines
1/4 pint (150ml) oil
2 oz (50g) butter or margarine
1 medium onion
4 tomatoes
2 tbsp (30ml) wholemeal flour
1/4 pint (142ml) milk
1 garlic clove, crushed
1/2 tsp (2.5ml) basil
1/2 tsp (2.5ml) oregano
Salt and pepper to taste
3 tbsp (45ml) parmesan cheese
3 tbsp (45ml) wholemeal breadcrumbs
Chopped parsley to garnish

Method
1. Cut the potatoes into large dice and cook in boiling water for about 10 minutes until just tender. Drain, reserving 1/2 pint (300ml) of cooking water.

2. Dice the aubergines and chop the onions and tomatoes.

3. Heat the oil and sauté the aubergines until golden and tender.

4. Melt half the butter and sauté the onion until transparent. Add the tomatoes, stir in the flour and cook for 1 minute.

5. Add the potato water, milk, garlic, herbs and seasoning. Bring to the boil, reduce heat and simmer for 15-20 minutes.

6. Spoon the potatoes and aubergines into a warmed serving dish. Spoon over the tomato sauce.

7. Mix together the breadcrumbs and Parmesan cheese and sprinkle over the sauce. Dot with the remaining butter.

8. Place in the oven at 200°C, 400°F, Gas Mark 6 for about 20 minutes until heated through. Sprinkle with chopped parsley.

A DAD'S LIFE IS A LOT LIKE TENNIS

There is nothing like a good lop. The therapeutic effect of pottering around the garden with the loppers is good for the soul. I was active around the estate the other evening crunching through some marauding ash trees that had set up camp in the hedge under the cover of a murky spring. As I was slicing my way through the defiant young shoots, I became aware of an apparition heading down the path. It was a figure clad in blue dressing gown and pink slippers and it was wailing pathetically.

Behind it I spotted another manifestation. This took the form of a bespectacled young human with a broad grin on its face and brandishing two tennis rackets. The first spectre was soon identified as Brat Major and the wailing became intelligible as one of the most well used children's phrases, "It's not fair". The one bringing up the rear was, of course, Brat Minor who had conned me in an unguarded moment into playing tennis with him as soon as I had finished my labours.

When I say play tennis, this is not the sport recognised by the LTA. It is but a crude form of the official game, played on the back lawn of Fortress Haverson. There is no net and the boundary of the court is the flower beds. We never change ends and the game only concludes when the ball has been struck into a neighbour's garden. The activity consists of me lobbing the ball gently in the direction of my enthusiastic young opponent. He then smashes it back, a good fifteen yards out of my reach, while leaping all over the place claiming he has just executed a cross court pass of Wimbledon-style perfection.

The reason for the pre-match scene the other evening involving Brat Major was that she considered my actions a gross violation of parental fair play to be offering to indulge in a game with her brother and not her.

I marched menacingly towards them clutching the loppers as if I was about to perform an amputation. I pointed out to Brat Major that she had been sent home from school ill. She had a headache and a temperature and her mother, who, as we all realise, knows best, had ordered her to bed early. Hence the dressing gown and slippers.

After much argument and wild promises from me that I would make good the situation just as soon as she felt better, Brat Major was finally persuaded to bed. In fact she went rather sharpish when Mrs H discovered her outside in her night clothes. To her chagrin the tennis match went ahead and I suffered a crushing defeat in a match that would have had John MacEnroe suffering apoplexy at the flagrant flouting of the rules.

I should have known better. It is a fact of life that with two children one has to play it straight down the middle. What one has, the other has to have and in exactly the same proportion. I have seen the whole family crouched, like atomic scientists, round the last Mars Bar in the house to make sure that it is being cut in half with the utmost precision to ensure that neither brat is disadvantaged in volume of chocolate.

Sometimes it is our own fault when we end up with only one of a particular thing. Have you ever tried to divide a bag of crisps equally between two vultures? And why do manufacturers supply those small cartons of juice in packs of three? You always wind up with an odd one. It is impossible for two children to share a carton of the sticky stuff. One grabs it from the other squeezing the container in the process. A jet of juice describes a gentle arc before coming to rest down the front of a clean tee shirt.

When they were younger and adoring relatives gave them pocket money, exactly the same coins had to be given to each of them. It was years before they accepted that a single gold coin could be equal to a handful of shiny silver ones.

The other night, Brat Minor slept round at a friends. Brat Major immediately demanded that a friend be fetched to sleep with her "to make up for what he's getting". I replied that as her brother wore glasses, we should, according to her logic, hasten to an optician to secure a pair for her as she was most certainly being hard done by.

I just can't win, rather like playing tennis with Brat Minor. Mind you, I suppose I could get round that one if I spirit away his tennis racket. A couple of good hacks with the loppers should do it.

A SHORT BOUT OF SLUM CLEARANCE

I hate decorating at the best of times. It's not so much the decorating, it's all the preparation work – clearing the room and filling up all the cracks that have mysteriously appeared since the last lick of paint. And why is it that just as I get started with the painting, I discover a hole in the plaster that surely wasn't there when I had the filler out?

There is one thing worse than just decorating and that is decorating Brat Minor's squat. It has been long overdue for redecorating and I have been putting it off, but finally I had to bite the bullet and do it. I shall most probably need some form of counselling after spending the best part of three days amid his memorabilia and weaponry.

I don't know what he gets up to in there. It took so much filler to repair all the little chips in the paintwork. Some of it is due to the regular changing of posters but I think a large proportion of the damage is caused when he has a ball up there or is locked in battle with some imaginary invading alien.

It must come from some planet where the inhabitants have no sense of smell.

First to be moved was his chest of drawers. This caused his entire armoury to plunge to the floor. There were swords, axes and guns everywhere, not to mention a series of holes in the wall where his trusty weapons had been roughly discarded after various battles. Bits of Lego got under foot and his favourite ankle-spraining trap, the rogue marble, all but had me on my back.

Moving his bed revealed two long-lost arrows and a small group of dinosaurs that his mother believed to be extinct. The reason why they have been having difficulty in completing a game of cards was also explained. The Jack of Spades and Clubs were in the custody of the dinosaurs.

I had free access to his room as he was away for the weekend at camp with the Cubs. His worried mother had packed him off with all the necessary gear and changes of clothes in accordance with Akela's list of instructions. Akela had sent to each young camper a set of rules compiled with his usual wry humour. "You can bring some sweets. Akelas like all sweets and eat huge quantities of them. At this camp there will be lots of Akelas."

Turns were to be taken at washing up so Brat Minor had to have a tea towel. Usually, he is conspicuous by his absence when this chore is being performed.

Also, Akela was quite explicit on the subject of washing. "I am sorry but you will be having a wash during the camp."

Even Brat Minor would be expected to cleanse himself. This was just as well as he had to share a tent with five others. These five have now experienced to some degree what it is like to spend a night in Brat Minor's squat. First-hand reports tell that it took him less than 24 hours to recreate the atmosphere of his home sleeping quarters.

It's a good job he didn't unzip his sleeping bag.

Akela also had rules for going to bed. "When you go to bed I would be grateful if you would wear something – even if you do not at home. If you need to get up in the night the toilet is not in the tent. The thought of you running to the toilet with no clothes on is already giving me nightmares and it is not fair to wake others up while you are looking for your pants."

What a prospect! A naked Brat Minor treading all over his slumbering chums as he fumbles for his unsavoury underpants before lurching off into the early morning mist in search of relief.

I am told that last weekend was the best for weather so far this summer. I wouldn't know. I spent most of the time on my slum regeneration project.

I emerged exhausted late on Sunday afternoon with the scars of battle still visible. Gloss on the glasses, emulsion in the hair and temper frayed from the odd inconvenience that happens to the hapless decorator, like treading on the carpet with paint on the bottom of the shoes.

I cleaned myself up and we retrieved a tired young Cub from his camp.

As I tucked him into bed that night, he turned to me and uttered words that made me, shall we say, a trifle tense. He spoke to me as an adult might to a child. Oblivious to his sparkling fresh surroundings, he asked patronisingly: "And what did you do this weekend while I was away?"

SOMEHOW I HAVE GAINED A REPUTATION

I seem to have attracted some sort of reputation of having a penchant for the hop. I was wondering just how this might have come about when a couple of incidents recently gave me the huge clue that my loyal family may have something to do with it.

It was some time in the run up to last weekend that the first comment was made. I was tucking into a healthy bowl of muesli when Brat Major plonked herself down beside me and said thoughtfully: "You had two cans of beer last night."

I thanked her for pointing this out and then asked her how she knew. It transpired that she had frisked the waste bin to gain this information. I thought no more about it until Saturday when a chain of events led me to the conclusion that she must have spread the word about her dad's drink problem.

Last weekend was busy for school events. On Saturday it was the First School fete. As we are no longer inflicting any offspring on this establishment, we thought it safe to go. In fact Mrs H, clad in Victorian below stairs gear, was assisting with the teas. She had left early with the Brats to do her tour of duty. I was going to follow later having taken the opportunity to wallow in front of the Test Match. However, the English wickets began to tumble so to avoid depression I set off for the school.

When I arrived, I offered my admission fee and, as he handed me my lucky programme, the chap on the gate dropped his voice and confided: "There's a beer tent in this year. It's in the far corner. We haven't advertised the fact."

"Oh," I said eagerly. "Just letting selected people know eh?" He nodded knowingly. As I made my way round the side of the school I bumped into someone I knew.

"You'll be pleased," he greeted me. "There's a beer tent this year." I was beginning to get a complex by now. To make it less obvious, I did the casual tour of the stalls and caught the end of the gymnastic display. Keeping well away from the beer tent I headed for the teas where Mrs H was being assisted by Brat Major. The dear girl was doling out the cream teas. I had one, even though I knew where the fingers that were dolloping the cream on the scones had been.

I briefed Mrs H on the beer tent and suitably replete I set out again. By sheer coincidence I assure you, I found myself heading in the general direction of the canvas watering hole. I thought I was unobserved but I was spotted by the old enemy, our former neighbour GBH.

"Hey, Neil!" she bawled in her own subtle way. "Look, there's a beer tent this year." I hastened over and engaged her in polite conversation so she couldn't embarrass me further. She was of course already drinking. For a time I resisted all urges to grab a pint but ended up slinking into the tent like a junky going to meet his supplier.

I melted into the crowd and wandered around clutching my pint. Suddenly a voice with that hint of authority brought me back to earth. "What are you looking so miserable for?" It was Brat Controller of the First School. We chatted a while and then Mrs H arrived.

"He was only coming for a while," she announced to The Brat Controller. "But he seems to have spent quite a bit of time here since he found there was a beer tent. And he was so pleased when he found it was beer straight from the barrel and not the fizzy stuff out of the cans."

I was actually on my second pint at the time and stood there listening to all this with a stupid grin on my face so, if I have got a reputation, it's hardly surprising.

As we drifted home from the fete I was mulling over this worrying situation when something else clicked into place. The following day, Sunday, was the Middle School PTA Fathers' Day car treasure hunt and I recalled Mrs H on the phone making enquiries about the event.

"Oh, and what time does the bar open? Neil wants to know if he can get a pint when we get back." Great, even my own wife is trying to make sure I get a regular fix.

The final straw came on Fathers' Day when I was graciously receiving gifts from my adoring children. Brat Minor handed over his offering and then leaned close to impart what was clearly going to be a pearl of wisdom.

"I usually get you some beer but I didn't think I'd better this year."

SUPPORT AT LAST – AND FROM GBH!

As I drove down the road to Fortress H, I spotted a car in our drive. I recognised it immediately, but if I had any doubts, confirmation as to the owner reached my ears well before I arrived at the back door.

As I walked down the path I was greeted by the squawk of gossiping women. One was, of course, Mrs H. The other was the old enemy, our ex-neighbour, GBH.

Ah, but is she still the enemy? As I entered the house, the two of them were sitting at the kitchen table drinking coffee and nattering. To my amazement, GBH expressed some sympathy for me.

"Gosh, you look worn out," she observed as I staggered through the door. "Come on then," she said to Mrs H. "Make the poor chap a cup of coffee." Mrs H's reply was not actually drawn from the English language. It came out as the kind of noise a horse sometimes makes.

"Phwuhumph!" is about the nearest I can come up with to describe the contemptuous snort Mrs H let fly.

I took this to be a translated version of "You must be joking. He is quite capable of making himself a drink if he wants one. I'm not waiting on him." GBH continued to support my cause while bravely I bated Mrs H, pointing out that it was highly unlikely that she would be able to make me a cup of coffee. It had been so long since she made the last one, it was doubtful whether she could remember how I take it.

GBH couldn't come to terms with this. She pointed out that here was a weary chap who had had a hard day at work earning a crust and the least his wife could do was provide him with a bit of refreshment. Mrs H went to some lengths to point out that if I cared to iron my own shirts, cook my own tea, take my daughter to dancing and the host of other unsalaried things she does, she would readily put herself on standby to make me a cup of coffee.

I thanked GBH profusely for her support – indeed for actually being there. Had she not, there is no way I would have been allowed to sit down. It would have been a touch of the "I'm glad you're home. Could you just do... " Anyway, Mrs H is not "the little woman" type at all so I am quite used to fending for myself.

I remember a lady at work telling me once that she had the

following day off.

"Lucky you," I said. "Think of us here when you are having your lie in."

"I should be so lucky," she replied. "My husband has got to go in to work. By the time I've got him breakfast, packed his lunch and got him off to work, it will be too late to go back to bed."

I should be so lucky too. The chances of Mrs H being able to drag herself out of bed before me are about as likely as Brat minor repaying a debt. And until someone invents the self-pouring packet of muesli and Tupperware come up with the bottomless lunch box, I'm on my own first thing in the morning.

I'd better be careful here or she may latch on to this and leave me entirely to my own devices which would not be a good idea. There are things I just don't understand. Take the other night for instance when I was spotted heading for the dirty linen basket with my blue sweatshirt.

"Oh no," exclaimed Mrs H in absolute frustration. "I've just put a blue wash in!" Clearly I had done something tantamount to breakdown in roadworks on the M25 in rush hour.

Wracked with guilt for reasons I couldn't comprehend, I offered to wear the sweatshirt for a few more days. Did she want me to scout round the house for a few more blue clothes to make up another wash? Perhaps the Brats could help. "No don't bother," she said grudgingly.

I could have done with some more help from GBH but even that new-found support had a sting in the tail. We bumped into her a few days later and I was moved to thank her for rallying to my cause.

To my amazement she took up the cudgel again. Wheeling around on Mrs H she said: "You should pamper him more." Mrs H grinned slyly and made it clear that, in her opinion, I hadn't done so badly throughout our married life.

"Yes, I know," said GBH "but his needs have changed." Then came the killer. "After all, he's a lot older now."

LURED INTO TROUBLE AT THE LOCAL PUB

As soon as I opened my mouth I knew I would regret it. Foolishly, I had offered to lend a hand with the odd Cubs' activity if Akela ever needed an extra pair of hands. When he said he could use some help at the local pub at 7 pm on the Friday night I was convinced I had made the right decision.

This sounded right up my street. Clearly things had moved on since my days in the Cubs. There must be a Drinker's Badge now and I was required to give a demonstration or perhaps even to test those hoping to gain their award.

Alas no, it was Akela's cunning way of getting me hooked. He brought me back to earth when he let me into the secret that the Cubs were going round the village on a treasure hunt, finishing up in the pub's gardens for a family barbecue. What he needed was some gullible parent to assist with the cooking.

Now, I have never subjected a burger to a grilling on a barbecue in my life so I summoned the fountain of all knowledge, Mrs H. But we had actually stumbled across something in which she has no experience either.

We arrived in good time and stood with another charcoal novice staring nervously at the cold barbecue. Our confidence surged when Akela strode into view carrying all the necessary gear. This same confidence diminished gradually over the next 45 minutes as all he succeeded in creating was an awful lot of smoke.

Fortunately some experts turned up and got the furnace going. I was allowed to cut the rolls and dispense the tomato sauce. Mrs H meanwhile tried her hand at the cooking. Every so often she would thrust her glass at me with the instruction to fill it up. This was an order that I was not unwilling to carry out. Well, while I was going I thought I might as well fill my glass up too.

Mrs H appeared to be doing quite well. I asked her what the two round bits of wood on the grill were for. "Oh," she confessed. "They're a couple of burgers I was making sure were properly done." Her fellow chefs later let is be known that in her enthusiasm Mrs H had also cremated a couple of innocent sausages when she demonstrated less than skilful use of the tongs and stuffed them through a convenient gap in the grill into the cinders.

Brat Major was assisting me with the roll-cutting when Akela came into view. She watched in awe as the harassed leader downed his pint in one and went about his duties of investing new Cubs and conducting a noisy Grand Howl. Conversation with him became hopeless after that. Every time I spoke to him he answered with "Mine's a pint."

There were no complaints from our customers. In case any of them were incapable of complaining through food poisoning, a quick sweep of the gardens revealed no one slumped under a bush clutching their stomach. We even sampled the fare ourselves in front of the punters with much exaggerated lip slapping to demonstrate the quality of our efforts.

Brat Minor arrived home from the barbecue with a sealed brown envelope. Ever the optimist, Akela had anticipated that boredom might well set in over the summer break so he had come up with a few ideas that would occupy the young holidaymakers and help them work towards more badges.

For the Cub Scout Award, Brat Minor and his chums were urged to "Keep a diary of good turns for a week, showing how you have helped other people." The Cub Scout Handbook defines a good turn as "a special job you do for someone that you might not normally do."

The potential here for Brat Minor is, therefore, enormous. He has tried it before and I must say it stretched him considerably. To the point where he was recording as a good turn the fact that he went to bed when told without causing his mother grief.

I shall watch with interest as he strives towards his Adventure Award. This badge has a section "Looking After Yourself". One of the exercises is to "Show that you can keep your room tidy." Just entering Brat Minor's squat is an adventure in itself. In fact, I am thinking about contacting Spielberg to see if he wants to film an Indiana Jones epic in there.

The barbecue escapade was not wasted. I did learn one thing from it. Akela has provided me with a useful answer to throw at Mrs H when her orders come raining in.

"Neil, for goodness sake when are you going to get round to decorating our bedroom?"

"Mine's a pint."

SILENCED BY A FAMILIAR PHRASE

One of Mrs H's favourite phrases is "Are you listening to me?" This is trundled out when I appear to be less than riveted while she is passing on some startling information such as the greengrocer didn't have any fresh aubergines. I am supposed to stop whatever I am doing and pay attention. Lots of eye contact to show I am absorbing the earth-shattering revelations. Sometimes she'll throw in a checking question, "What did I just say?" When the boot is on the other foot and it is I who am trying to pass on some news, she always seems to be distracted and I get put in the queue.

She will hold up a threatening hand to silence me. There is something on the radio that has caught her attention, she is in the middle of calculating how many equal portions her freshly cooked flapjack will make and the washing machine is churning noisily away. If I am brave enough to let slip some signs of impatience, she uses one of her other favourite phrases as she shunts me into a siding. "I just can't compete!"

I do find it frustrating sometimes. The other night I came home bubbling over with enthusiasm, eager to tell her some news. My little face was glowing with excitement but every time I spoke I got put on hold.

"Hey, guess what? I went into a shop today and..."

"Just a minute...will you two wash your hands and come and eat your food NOW! Sorry what were you saying?"

"I went into the shop and ..."

"Now listen to them. They can't even wash their hands without arguing. SHUT UP! Sorry, go on."

"I went..."

"Will you two come here NOWWW! It's no good, you'll have to tell me later." At this point I leave the room. Later never comes, I am accused of going off in a huff and out comes that phrase. "It's not my fault they were being difficult so I couldn't concentrate on what you were saying. I just can't compete!"

I should know better by now as this happens so often. The trouble is, I haven't updated my manual of house rules. The house rules at Fortress H are so complex they would make an ideal subject for a GCSE. Part of the problem is that the rules are like triffids, they seem to keep on growing. For example, we had an addition thrown in the other night that was quite new to me.

One of the washing up laws is as follows: the washer-upper shall wipe all kitchen worktops in order that the dryer-upper shall have a clean surface upon which to place the bits and pieces that have been dunked in Fairy Liquid. Usually that is no problem because the washer-upper and the dryer-upper are one and the same person. Me.

The other tea time, there was help in the form of a reluctant Brat Major. Dutifully I wiped the worktop and washed up a plate. My grudging assistant grabbed it precariously, dried it and turned to put in on the work surface.

"WAIT!" bawled Mrs H. She was lucky her startled daughter managed to cling on to the bit of crockery. "The work surface has not dried yet. You'll be putting clean things on a wet top."

I failed to see the problem. As long as the surface was clean did it really matter? Anyway, the difficulty was soon solved. Brat Major seized the opportunity to disappear, claiming that she was just popping outside while the worktop dried. She was not seen again for some time by which time I had completed the washing up, the worktop was dry and I had done the wiping up.

Sometimes you can get away with breaches of Fortress discipline simply by denying everything. No one has yet owned up to an act of petty larceny from an unattended tin of sweets. That means nobody saw the offence take place. The trouble is, if you are spotted, there are a couple of grasses among the inmates who will stitch you up if they think it will ingratiate them with she who sits in judgement.

Having complained at the proliferation of house rules, perhaps there should be an additional edict to sort out my communication problems. Maybe I should be allocated quality talk time in return for which I would desist from glazed looks and perfunctory grunts when Mrs H engages me in conversation.

I do wonder why Mrs H puts me in second place when I am bursting to impart some news. Could it be that my gossip is even more boring than the harrowing tales of fruitless quests for elusive aubergines? Perhaps, to use the words of Mrs H, I just can't compete.

NO LET-UP ONCE I'M WRONG

There are times when Mrs H leaves me speechless. She has come out with some pearlers in her time but this latest one takes some beating. She had asked me to put some things into the loft. I had already put one lot away but she claimed I had only done half the job. I insisted that I hadn't realised there was more to do but she was adamant that her instructions had been quite clear. And then she said it. She stated that she had not mentioned these other things for the loft again because, "I am not the sort of wife to go on and on about things."

That really is rich! If I step out of line and it is necessary for Mrs H to administer one of her rallying speeches to put me right, it becomes rather like a party political broadcast. I have learned to stand quietly and listen to the wisdom. I do this in the hope that if I demonstrate that I am contrite, that I am taking on board all the good advice that she is dispensing and declare that I will never again give her cause for discontent, that will be an end to the matter. This is not usually the case.

Having made her point over such issues as my inability to shut the toilet window before we go out, she will disappear. I get on with whatever it is I was doing but sure enough, within a few minutes she is back having another go.

"You'd be the first to complain if someone broke in and stole the video. We haven't got much that's worth stealing but it's all we can afford." The subject will then be touched on periodically throughout the day. I will hear the Brats being briefed on it. "And don't leave the backdoor unlocked like your father does with the toilet window."

Finally I will hear her manage to work it into conversation when she is on the 'phone to one of her mates. "Yes, I know. I said to Neil, if he keeps leaving the toilet window open, we'll be next."

This seems grossly unfair. I don't do it to her. I could find loads of things about her to go on and on about. Take her toad-in-the-hole for instance. It's not stodgy and we all like it but when she cooks it, the same thing always happens. We had it for dinner only the other night. There we were, all the inmates of Fortress Haverson, seated around the dining table salivating furiously in anticipation of Mrs H's toad-in-the-hole when bingo, the jinx struck.

"Oh no! It's done it again. Why does the pudding always stick to the bottom of the tin. It's the only thing I make that does that." There followed a scraping and gouging as she used almost her entire range of kitchen tools to persuade the pudding to end its relationship with the baking tin. By the time it arrived on the plate, it was what you might call MFI Toad-in-the-hole. Self assembly.

There was the usual banter as we ate our meal. "If it sticks to the tin like that, what on earth is it doing to our stomachs!" But I knew there was worse to come – for me anyway. The tin had to be washed up and we all know whose job that is. On this particular occasion, Mrs H left it to soak. About an hour later I had a go at it and managed to get the outer crust off. I left it to soak a bit longer then had another try. Mrs H heard me scrubbing and took pity on me. She suggested we leave it in water overnight. I favoured giving it a swift rinse in Hydrochloric Acid.

Eventually I was able to reveal the bottom of the tin. I am also wise to the fact that I must prevent the scrapings going down the plug hole. Mix this stuff with water and the sink might be sealed up like Tutankhamun's tomb.

In fact I have asked Mrs H for the secret of her recipe for batter pudding. It would make ideal filler for the walls when I am decorating or seal a leaky radiator. I could say more but I am not the sort of chap to labour a point.

Not like Mrs H, though she still insists she does not go on and on. "If I did," she protests, "the bedroom would have been decorated years ago." I tell her, the more she persists about things the more it builds up my resistance to them. Mind you, perhaps that applies to her toad-in-the-hole. She has fed it to us so regularly, we have become immune to it.

BRAT MINOR THINKS AT HIS OWN PACE

I had hoped that the school holidays would have enabled the vague Brat Minor to rest his brain and get it in gear for the new term. Alas no, it seems that his cerebral cogs continue to turn at his own comfortable pace. My hopes had remained high until I 'phoned home late one afternoon.

Mrs H was coming into the city with the two young inmates and she couldn't remember the time of the bus. We arranged that I would telephone at about the time she thought they would be leaving to make sure they were on target to catch the bus so I wasn't left jaywalking in St Stephen's. Brat Minor would be stationed by the phone to tell me their time of arrival and where we were to meet. I rang at the appointed hour and he answered almost instantly.

"We found a bus timetable in the museum," he announced. Museum? I had to admit that I couldn't recall a museum in the village. Well, there is my wardrobe. That's got a few relics in it but other than that I was stumped. Then a voice in the background prompted him.

"Oh, I mean the library," he corrected himself before launching into the rest of the message. "And we'll....we'll...what are we going to do?" He appealed to his prompter for help. Finally I got the gist of things. Later, I wished I hadn't. I met them on schedule and was promptly handed 3 bags containing clothes from various stores. Brat Minor and I were dispatched to obtain refunds for the lot while the females swanned around the city looking for replacements.

A few days after this we had another howler form the dreamy Brat Minor. He arrived home from school one night with the news that they had been told to copy their timetable from the blackboard. In spite of a valiant effort, the dozy creature had failed to copy it out before it was removed from the board. To add to the woes of our luckless scholar, he then mislaid his half-finished effort.

By constantly asking him all the way to school, to repeat what he had to do, Mrs H managed to program him to borrow a timetable so he could copy it out at home. Then his luck changed. He stumbled across someone else's half complete timetable. Not being as daft as he may seem, Brat Minor put it in his schoolbag and brought it home thinking he might finish it off. His mother had other ideas but her efforts to obtain a timetable from his classmates so he could do a fresh copy proved fruitless.

On Sunday night, just as he was resigned to confessing all to his teacher, inspiration suddenly flashed across his face.

"Do you know, " he babbled excitedly. "I think I recognise the writing on that half-finished timetable I brought home."

"Really," said Mrs H enthusiastically. "Whose is it?"

"Mine," came the triumphant reply.

I suppose I shouldn't be surprised really. He doesn't stand much chance when you consider the workings of his mother's grey matter. She bought him some new Y-fronts for the autumn term. She got out the marker pen and carefully labelled them – with his sister's name. With his track record, it wouldn't have been long before he lost a pair. Can you imagine his embarrassment if they had been held up in the changing room after swimming and the name read out for the rightful owner to claim them?

I thought all this forgetfulness was supposed to be a sign of age. Actually, that is a sore point at the moment. Last Saturday was the first hockey match of the season and I could have done without the comments I received from certain people in the village on the morning before I played. First I ran across our old friend GBH. Never one to miss an opportunity, she remarked hurtfully, "Don't you think you're a bit old for that sort of thing now?"

Mrs H was at the crimpers and I called in to deposit Brat Minor into her custody before leaving for the game. As I left the salon, the crimper waved a hair dryer at me and said with a smile that had more than a hint of sarcasm to it, "Take it easy this afternoon won't you."

As I lurched around the field in the teeming rain, I began to think they were right. Perhaps it was time to hang up the stick. And when I almost left my soaking kit on the changing room floor, I decided the mind really was going. Though it wouldn't have mattered if I had left my gear behind. I am sure Mrs H will have marked it. Mind you, I don't know with whose name.

GET US TO THE CHURCH ON TIME... PLEASE

My knuckles were white. I was gripping the steering wheel as if my life depended on it. In fact it, and the lives of the other inmates of Fortress Haverson, almost certainly did. We were on the M25 in a sea of vehicles which I can only describe as a moving traffic jam searching hungrily for a contraflow in an effort to get a mention on the radio travel bulletins.

Of course, things went beyond just coping with the traffic. Life has to throw in a few extra wobblies to keep you on your toes. We were off to a attend a wedding at Maidenhead in Berkshire. Yes, you've guessed it, we were late in leaving. In spite of careful preparation the night before we were soon half an hour behind schedule.

The alarm went off on time and I nudged Mrs H into consciousness. We launched into our pre-travel plan which included, for me, a trip to the crimper. This involved not just a haircut but a profound discussion on the difference between the way men and women think. A dangerous topic in which to become embroiled when you have a female slashing away around your head with a pair of scissors.

I survived and, having shopped in the village, returned home to find things progressing nicely. But somehow time drifted away and one of the travellers was not ready as soon as the others. I am sure there is no need for me to identify which one. The result was that we left home in a state of mild panic which intensified when we hit the A11 and were forced to make our way to the Suffolk border without troubling the accelerator pedal unduly.

We had decided that two children could never make a journey of 150 miles and arrive at the other end with their clothes in pristine condition, especially if we stopped on route to grab some refreshment. The intention had been to get to our destination in good time where there was somewhere for them to change.

Our delayed start scuppered this. We gambled some of our precious time on a stop for a drink. This took longer than intended. Having said he was desperate to go to the toilet, Brat Minor failed to come up with the goods when given the opportunity. I waited for ages with him and eventually he performed but by then we had a real fear that we would not arrive in time to avoid the pair of them turning up at the wedding in jeans and T-shirts. There was no alternative but for them to change in the car.

So there we were, locked in combat with three lanes of motorists who seemed to think they were part of a herd of stampeding wildebeest. While I was trying to hold my own among this lot, Mrs H was trying to supervise the changing of two children from scruff gear into freshly laundered and pressed clothes. As she was in the front and they were in the back she performed this function largely through shouting at them.

Meanwhile Brat Major was haranguing me for being in the middle lane so that she could be viewed, half clothed, from both the inside and outside lanes. My protestations that I had no choice as I was boxed in on all sides failed to appease her dignity.

I should point out that throughout the operation both of them were firmly in the control of their seat belts. This of course foxed Brat Minor. Having struggled into his shirt with the help of several bellows from his mother as he all but caused the sleeves to part company with the rest of the garment, he began to button himself in with the shirt wrapped round the seat belt.

Eventually they were dressed and we actually arrived in very good time. We alighted from the car having got lost in the one way system to be greeted with the usual, "Did you have a good journey?"

The answer was a typically British understatement. We had left late and driven the first forty miles in driving rain at little more than 40 miles per hour. I am probably on video loitering in the gents loos at the South Mimms Service Area and we had travelled the notorious M25 in a mobile changing room.

"Not bad at all," we heard ourselves saying. "Made good time considering."

The wedding was super. The bride looked gorgeous, the groom was wreathed in smiles and we caught up on all the family gossip. Finally we hit the trail for Norfolk. A tired Brat Minor piped up that he thought it would be a good idea to stop on the way home. We did – but not at South Mimms.

ALL IS QUIET ON THE FORTRESS FRONT

Like most married couples, Mrs H and I have had our share of rows. They are like those humps in the road that control traffic. They check your speed along the rat-run of married life. Happily we're on the open road at the moment but that's always a worrying sign. If things are running smoothly, usually it means we are about ripe to turn down a side road and have a belter.

I suppose there isn't a good or bad time to have a row but they do seem to come at the most inconvenient moments. The prime time for a bust-up is either late at night when one or the other just wants to go to sleep or, worse still, when you are going out for the evening. She is irritable because she can't decide what to wear and he is tetchy because he has to drive and therefore can't drink.

These particular arguments usually build up to a climax which comes in the form of an ultimatum. "That's it. Go on your own. I'm damned if I want to go with you when you are in a mood like this." The other partner is seized by a fit of mild panic realising they would be left to arrive solo and explain where their other half is. Lots of concessions come on to the negotiating table at this stage and a compromise is usually reached.

After she has carried out some hasty repairs to her make-up to camouflage the effect of active tear ducts, there follows a tense, agonisingly silent car journey to the party. It's rather like being in a plane at 12,000 feet waiting to make your first parachute jump.

Once the door bell is rung at the end of this frosty trip, the human being reveals its chameleon qualities. As the door is opened, the hostile couple greet their hosts wreathed in warm smiles and troop over the threshold exuding an aura of marital harmony. The illusion is perpetuated with ice-breaking phrases like, "Its ages since we have seen you. We were only saying in the car on the way over, weren't we dear?"

With a few sherbets under the belt, things begin to mellow. The irony comes later in the evening when our reconciled couple nudge each other knowingly as that pair in the corner start arguing over when to leave. She wants to stay in the hope of another dance with that guy with the earring and tight trousers while he wants to get home to catch Match of the Day.

Most rows seem to be about the same things and are quite forgettable. Indeed, Mrs H is always pointing out my capacity to learn absolutely nothing from what she considers to be the eminently sensible observations she makes about my failings.

She had a chuckle the other day as she recalled a ding dong we had in our early, pre-brat days. Now, you would think that if someone hurled a weighty piece of pottery at you then there is a reasonable chance the incident would warrant a permanent place in the memory. Mrs H claims that in an effort to communicate her displeasure she threw an ashtray at me but I cannot, for the life of me, remember the incident.

The argument may have been so insignificant that I have forgotten. It may be that I suffered severe concussion or that post trauma shock has caused my mind to reject all memories of it. Was I actually winning the argument and Mrs H decided the only way to gain the upper hand was to seize the nearest movable object and aim it in my direction? I certainly do not recall anything like it since. There has been door slamming and table thumping but I have not been the victim of Mrs H's "friendly fire".

Life in the trenches has indeed been quiet at Fortress H lately. Maybe it's because Brat Major is being particularly grumpy and that has deflected the focus from me. But I have a feeling aggro will be waiting if I pop my head over the parapet. I am a trifle worried that, having recalled her strategy from that previous battle, Mrs H may be moved to employ it next time she wishes to add a bit of clout to her argument.

She reckons she missed the target last time but her aim may have since improved. Fortunately, neither Mrs H nor I smoke so I haven't seen an ashtray about the place for years. Nevertheless, to be on the safe side perhaps I had better secure all objects that are suitable both to throw and cause pain.

I just hope we don't have a row after she has made toad-in-the-hole. That really could do me some damage.

AKELA TAKES HIS GRIM REVENGE

My occasional practice of Akela-bating through this column appears to have resulted in a battle of wills between me and the aforesaid cub leader. I have written about his drinking habits and his inability to light a barbecue. In response, he has sent out newsletters via the cubs to their parents in which he makes thinly disguised comments about yours truly.

In the most recent communiqué he casts doubt upon the accuracy of what is written in a local paper by a certain cub parent. He goes on to drop a broad hint that the dad in question ought to show his mettle by going to next year's camp.

I retaliated at the cubs fireworks party by expressing surprise that, in the absence of a guy, Akela had not volunteered to clamber to the top of the bonfire and get frazzled. After all, did he not look dressed for the part? In getting his own back, he has become remarkably subtle. Clearly, his strategy is to wear me down. In his latest move he targeted my blood pressure. It was a simple but cunning plan. He asked Brat Minor to carry the flag at the Remembrance Day Parade.

Now anyone who has attempted to share the same piece of hemisphere as Brat Minor will know that he can stumble over a grain of sand and cause apparently unattended bottles of milk to perform somersaults. To ask him to carry a standard on a parade and manoeuvre successfully along the aisles of the church is rather like asking Dracula to walk past a blood bank.

It was at the rehearsal the day before the event that I began to feel the tension building up. Brat Minor is not a giant among cubs and I feared the standard, which was at least twice his height, might overwhelm him. He succeeded in raising it to the upright position and joined the convoy on its voyage along the middle aisle of the church to run through the Receiving of the Standards ceremony. All bar one of the standard bearers negotiated the chandelier without incident. Yes, you can guess which one managed to give it a clout.

The rector took the flags at the altar and, after a few words of instruction, returned them to the bearers. I watched with some relief as Brat Minor and his two escorts embarked on the return journey. My relief was short-lived. He was carrying a completely different flag to the one with which he had set out.

After a quick exchange of flags it was off to rehearse the routine around the memorial. This passed without incident but when they were dismissed, Brat Minor was like a cork popping out of a champagne bottle. With flag at the horizontal he took flight and all but lanced the unsuspecting rector. I led our young hero away as the startled man of the cloth murmured something about The Charge of the Light Brigade.

Later that evening, I confessed to Mrs H that I didn't think I could survive the pressure of the live performance the following day. Brat Minor, on the other hand, remained largely unruffled. The strain on his bony little arms worried him not. Meanwhile his father had neck muscles that were in knots which certainly aren't in the Scout's manual.

The following morning, we got the eager standard bearer ready for his big moment. I rolled his scarf for him and he attached his woggle. Minutes later, Mrs H appeared and let fly a huge tut that sounded like a Wellington Boot being withdrawn from heavy mud. "I suppose your father did this." she muttered removing the scarf and starting again.

The parade set off with a brave Akela marching at the head of his pack. He was just feet from Brat Minor and well within striking distance. They arrived safely at the church and lined up for the Act of Remembrance. White knuckled, I watched as Brat Minor clung manfully to his flag. My stress intensified when a slight wind got up and the flags began to billow. Like a galleon leaving harbour, Brat Minor began to rock dangerously in the breeze.

As he lowered the flag during the Last Post I stifled a scream. He removed the flag from the carrier and, to give himself room to lower it, thrust the pole backwards. It was more by luck than judgement that an unsuspecting cub in the rear rank avoided the enjoyment of a levitating experience thanks to the sudden arrival of a flag pole between his legs.

After the parade, we collected Brat Minor from a triumphant Akela. Maybe I should go to that camp next summer to get my own back. Mind you, would either of us rest easily in our sleeping bags knowing that the other was busy scheming in the adjacent tent.

IT'S NOT THE SIZE THAT COUNTS

My ineptitude has just been shot into perhaps its sharpest perspective. I thought Mrs H had long since come to terms with my abysmal record but it seems she has been harbouring yet another Haversonism, just waiting for the opportunity to go public. But I suppose she does have a lot to put up with.

I have more DIY failures to my credit than Frank Spencer. I still put too much water in the frozen peas. I am impatient during the ballgown selection period prior to going out. I am unromantic. I buy her practical not personal things for her birthday. As if all that isn't enough to shatter the confidence of any man, I have now suffered this further devastating blow to my ego.

My potatoes are too small. It's true. I cannot even grow potatoes of sufficient size to please Mrs H.

The public humiliation came when someone kindly offered Mrs H some potatoes and she responded with quite unnecessary enthusiasm. "Oh yes please! Neil grew some but they're so small. They get on my wick."

I did my best. I prepared the soil with compost. Dug precision trenches according to the gospel of Readers Digest. To the millimetre I gently laid the seed potatoes the correct distance apart. As they grew I hoed the bindweed and moulded them up. Lovingly I watered them and what was my reward? Spuds the size of marbles.

I must say that, just lately, I seem to be coming in for more than my fair share of criticism from Mrs H. The other morning, when I had the day off, she breezed out of the house having reeled off a list of instructions. Usual sort of things. "Hang out the towels if it's not raining. Returf the lawn, install a new central heating system and don't forget to get the towels back in again if does rain."

Some three hours later she returned to assess my progress. She peered down the garden and I smiled with satisfaction as the towels flapped happily in the wind. The smile was soon wiped from my face. I really didn't think it possible to go too far wrong in simply hanging out the washing but can you believe it? I hadn't done it to Fortress guide-lines.

"I'll have to go and move them. Just look. You've got two of them wrapping themselves round that rusty linen prop and that tea towel is stuck in the apple tree. I don't know." She swept out of the back door let go a huge sigh of patient suffering upon which rode words of further criticism. "And look how you've pegged them. They're far too tight."

Mrs H has been in a particularly bullish mood all round recently. Fortunately not all her wrath has been vented on me. She took a sideswipe at society in general the other day. Mind you, I was the one to set her off. Quite innocently, I mentioned in passing how much easier it is to add up sums of money with decimalisation than it was with pounds, shillings and pence. This set her off. I'd obviously touched a nerve.

"I don't like it," she scoffed. "I don't know why we had to change. I liked our pounds, shillings and pence. I don't like metric either. They measure up for carpets in metres but sell it by the square yard. And I don't see why we should change gallons for litres."

I know better than to argue when Mrs H is having a go at the system. Before I know it, all the ills of the country will be my fault. I personally will have been responsible for taking us into Europe.

Having said all that, I do believe I may have finally cracked one of the age old problems. It's that one where three orders are rattled off in quick succession and no matter which one I choose to do first it should have been one of the other two.

The answer came to me the other night as I was watching an American cop show. The squad room was full of officers when the captain walked in. "There's an incident on 1423rd street." Nobody moved. "It's a code 3." Immediately they all leapt up and rushed out. It's so simple. All Mrs H has to do is to put my orders in priority by giving them a code.

"The children are fighting. Sort them out – code 3. The rubbish needs emptying – code 8. Get me some potatoes so I can do your tea – code 109."

Talking of potatoes again, after Mrs H's hurtful remarks I have vowed not to grow any next year. I can't think why she finds small potatoes such a problem . Besides, I'm sure I've heard somewhere that size isn't important

MRS H COMES OUT A NEW WOMAN

The bathroom door opened and Mrs H's head appeared. "I am going to have a bath. I don't want anybody to disturb me. I am going to relax , read my book and come out a new woman."

Immediately I asked if I could contribute to the specification of this refurbished female. My request was answered with a snort. The door was closed and Archimedes Principle was put to the test once again as Mrs H lowered herself into the steaming bath.

After some splashing around, the noise from the bathroom died down as Mrs H settled into her book. Meanwhile, I began to wonder just what I would change about her if I really did want an updated model. I must confess I was hard pressed to find much. She still looks good. Hang on, does that sound as though she ought to be showing signs of wear and tear? Perhaps I should phrase that differently. She remains naturally attractive and this is only enhanced by her youthful outlook on life.

Undoubtedly she motivates me to do things I would not otherwise do. Whether this is through fear or her natural leadership qualities I am not sure. And without her my wardrobe would be merely an amalgam of apparel awaiting the blessed release of a jumble sale. And just think, if I had not married Mrs H, I may never have been introduced to the mouth watering delights of the Aubergine Bake.

Anyway, she is much wiser than I in all matters - except maybe one. This is the area of the Fortress Motorpool. She steers well clear of vehicle maintenance. In fact, my extremely limited knowledge of the internal combustion engine makes me look like a qualified mechanic by comparison. She knows where the petrol goes in and that it has to be paid for but when it comes to putting it into practice she takes a back seat.

I must say, she is improving. The car was due for a service the other week so I rang Spannerman to warn him that I would be in not only for a service but with some of Mrs H's quaint instructions. She delivers these in highly technical jargon such as "Do brakes", whatever that means.

"Tell him there is a squeak when I start and stop," she said. I was about to make a crack about trapped mice in the carburettor when she floored me by adding, "I think it might be the fan-belt." I was impressed. This was not an unreasonable diagnosis. I delivered this message to Spannerman along with my request for him to check out the radio speakers which were distorting the sound.

The radio is of no concern to Mrs H. She claims never to have it on as it distracts her from her driving. I could understand this if it wasn't for the fact that she completes most of her journeys with a couple of small humans who spend most of the trip attempting, within the constraints of their seat-belts, to execute a screaming mugging on each other.

Spannerman is also charged with maintaining the car driven by our trusty Brat Warden. She who is prepared to be locked up alone in the house with the Brats while Mrs H and I recharge our batteries in the outside world. However, she has heard me say things like "spark plug" and "windscreen wiper" so assumes I must have some idea about cars. In fact the other night, when the starter motor jammed, I was invited to have a go at it. Having had the same trouble myself, I knew the remedy.

"Stick it in second gear and I'll rock it back and forwards," I instructed. She hopped in and I heard the gears crunching. "OK," she confirmed and I gave the car a heave forward. It lumped into a bike at the end of the garage. Hastily I pulled the other way. Suddenly I realised I was working my way back up the drive. With the car in gear it should move only inches.

"Are you sure it's in gear?" I shouted to the Brat Warden who was seated comfortably in the car while I was doing all the hard work. She confirmed it was and I shoved again. The bike received another solid nudge and I pulled the other way again only to find myself back pedalling up the drive once more.

Then, from the safety of the car, a plaintiff voice said, "Will it help if I take my foot off the clutch?"

I recounted the story to Mrs H expecting her to see the funny side. Instead she said with some concern, "You're lucky pushing it didn't make the engine start."

No dear, that's a bump start when you have a flat battery. Why don't you go and have another bath?

SOME MACHO LAMBS ARE IN DISGUISE

Mrs H and I were in a pub one night talking to this guy we knew who was waiting for his wife. He was pontificating loudly on all sorts of things. Pausing only to quaff his pint he made his views known on marriage, politics and the price of aubergines. Then his wife walked in. Immediately he was transformed into a wimp. We hardly exchanged a word with him for the rest of the time he was in the pub – which wasn't very long. Soon, he was told he was going home and he meekly followed his wife out of the bar.

This does make me wonder just how many of all the other machos we see and hear around are mere lambs when under tight domestic control of the like that prevails at Fortress H. Only a couple of weeks ago, I unwittingly revealed just how strong the Fortress umbilical chord is.

I was with some team mates in the bar after a hockey match when someone enquired after the well-being of Mrs H. My reaction was instant. I looked straight at my watch. The very mention of my good lady's name sent the brain into self-preservation mode. Was I running late? How much had I had to drink? What excuse should I use this time?

This did not go unnoticed by the populous in the bar who drew this instinctive reaction to my attention with great mirth. But how many of them, I wondered, were also going through the same thought processes?

Actually, I could use some help from a fellow servile. I don't know what to buy Mrs H for Christmas. I am absolutely stuck. Over the last twenty odd years I have attempted to be innovative with my present buying. Take the time I included a salad spinner among my gifts. Gosh, what an old romantic I am. But this year nothing comes to mind.

I thought I'd ask Mrs H what she wanted but she wasn't too much help. Apart from the usual, "I like to be surprised" she came out with the hardy annuals. A CD, chocolates, clothes. Ah, now clothes, that's a definite no no. I've tried that and shopping alone for clothes for Mrs H is more stressful than being dragged round with her. Why should it be so embarrassing?

The first time I went solo, I took a deep breath, marched into the shop and ordered something flimsy. It was a bit like the Harp TV advert where the assistant holds up the underwear and, to the man's acute embarrassment, shouts to her supervisor for a bigger size. In my case she connected various fasteners, held up the garment for all to see and asked, "Is that all right sir?"

The time it took to put the underwear into a bag, for me to pay for it and leave the store seemed as long as a Party Political Broadcast. The sick thing is, as we eager husband soon learn, this type of garment soon disappears into a drawer and doesn't see the light of day again.

Undaunted, I did try again. This time, after subtle questioning, I established that she wanted a blouse. I remember shuffling round the store like a shop-lifter. Having identified the blouse on the rack, I was waiting for the check-out to clear. Unfortunately, when it became free, I was some way from the particular rack with the blouse on it. Nevertheless, I took off like Linford Christie, grabbed the blouse and raced to the till.

Fate was against me. By the time I had circumnavigated strategically placed rails loaded with ladies' apparel, it seemed that half the female population of Norwich was queuing to pay. I fell in line clutching a black chiffon blouse and feeling myself becoming hotter and hotter. By the time I arrived at the till my bottle was completely gone. In an attempt to recover my composure, I just had to say something.

"If SHE wants to change it can SHE bring it back?" I demanded in a voice that only made matters worse. Driven by near hysteria, it climbed an octave.

I received a knowing smile in return. The blood was pounding in my ears but I am sure the girl said, "Yes, of course YOU can." At least Mrs H did wear the blouse.

I see the underwear shops have Gentlemen's evenings now. Chaps can go along and circulate freely without embarrassment. I'd probably turn up in disguise and try to slip in unnoticed.

And I know my luck. Just as I arrived, Mrs H would happen to walk past. Explain your way out of that one Haverson.

WE GO LIKE LABRADORS TO THE SLAUGHTER

I have been worried all Christmas. The cause of my concern was the letter in the EDP on Friday December 16th from Andrew Youngs of Bungay. Having read of my struggle for survival in the marriage stakes at Fortress H, Andrew raised the question, why did I and others like me get married in the first place? As a confirmed bachelor, he cannot understand why we go to the altar, fall on our swords and spend the rest of our lives living in fear.

It's not fear. We are like faithful Labradors. We are easily trained to come to heel and have a need to please. The only difference is that dogs are trained by rewarding them when they get it right. Their owners make a fuss of them. That part hasn't filtered through to the human version yet.

I just can't see how Andrew survives. He is drifting rudderless across the ocean of life. After a hard days graft, who stops him falling asleep in the armchair? And how does he know what time he is supposed to leave the pub? He could be there until closing time. That happened to me once. Fortunately the chap behind the bar offered a service to remind you. "Last orders," he shouted. Immediately I remembered that my last orders were to be home by 10.30 p.m. and I took off like lightning.

I bet Andrew has been outside in his slippers. You see, there is no guardian angel to call softly to him, "Oi! How many times have I told you. You'll ruin your slippers if you keep going to the dustbin in them."

How does he deal with his money? There he is on pay day with a wallet full of cash and no one to give it to. There is a serious danger here that he might spend it on things he wants. That would never do. Money is earned to be handed over for housekeeping and to buy useful things like mountains of cotton wool and innumerable pairs of tights.

I've seen the likes of Andrew at parties. They are the ones already there and well oiled by the time Mrs H and I arrive. How they must miss the opportunity marriage would give them of building up to the event as they wait for their good woman. Pacing up and down the hall, jangling the car keys and counting the stipples on the Artex ceiling.

Of course, another thing Andrew is denied, before headaches become a regular feature of married life, is all the pleasures that come with procreation. The elbow in the ribs that says it's your turn to get up and calm the wailing brat. Investing in petrol and time to operate a taxi service to run the little dears to all their extra-curricular activities. And having your family's darkest secrets trawled through the playground.

I had to find out just how serious a case Andrew is so I telephoned him – not only to find out how he survives but also, I thought he might appreciate an opportunity to use his phone. Without a woman in the house, the instrument probably stands idle for long periods. To establish how well he looks after himself, I asked him a simple checking question.

"Do you eat white bread?"

"Yes," he replied. "It's the only bread I eat."

"There you are," I announced with triumph. "You're not getting your roughage."

"But I like the taste," he protested.

"That's not the point," I informed him. "Enjoyment doesn't come into it. It's whether or not it's good for you that matters."

"We could meet up for a beer and talk about this," suggested Andrew. He just doesn't understand.

"Ah, that'll be a bit difficult," I replied. "What with Christmas, I've been given a fairly strict timetable." Could it be that I was losing the argument? "How about the new year?"

Andrew pointed out that it would have to be sooner rather than later. He has resigned his job and is off to seek his fortune in South Africa. "Something you married chaps can't do," he said with just the merest hint of smugness in his voice. All right, I admit defeat.

There was one obvious source of information as to why I got married. Mrs H. She wasn't too helpful. She greeted the question with that endearing snort of hers which sounds like a horse with sinusitis.

"If you don't know far be it from me to tell you." I must admit, it was me that suggested we got married. She didn't have me in an arm lock at the time.

Perhaps it's simply that chaps like Andrew have foresight. What he already knew, the likes of me don't find out until it's too late.

WASHING DAY AND I'M WRONG AGAIN

I must say I have been reassured by the reaction to my revelations a few weeks ago that I am incapable of hanging out the washing correctly. Judging by the letters page, it seems that I am far from alone in my ineptitude. However, I can report that I have now taken the art of clothes drying to a new low.

The misty, murky damp weather, such as we have at this time of year, is guaranteed to put Mrs H in a mood. It rankles with her that she cannot get her washing dry. If she hangs it outside, it comes in as wet as it went out. During the cold snap before Christmas, the washing froze. Everything came in as if it had overdosed on starch. Brat Minor's jeans were as stiff as a board. They often go into the wash in that state but having been declagged, do not usually reappear in the same condition.

The poor old tumble dryer cannot keep up so Mrs H falls back on the central heating system. Every radiator in Fortress H is draped with an assortment of socks, shirts and towels. My failure came when I was asked to assist with decorating the radiators.

Obediently, I hung some jeans over the one in the hall. Having completed my task, I stepped back to admire my handy work. There was a sound behind me like an articulated lorry releasing its air brakes.

"Turn those jeans round," admonished the source of the hissing. "They'll never dry like that without smelling. You must hang them so the thick part with the zips is next to the radiator." Brat Major walked by shaking her head sadly as if to say "Is he really my father?"

Brat Major is maturing by the day and is already taking on board all those quaint feminine habits that will one day drive her man to distraction. It seems that either she or her mother are continually emerging from the bathroom with dripping hair. At least Brat Major disappears to her bedroom to perform the drying operation. Mrs H does it in the North Wing where I am attempting to watch television.

My viewing is punctuated with hissed curses as she continually injects herself with those needle sharp plastic darts that hold the rollers in place. This I can live with but the hair dryer is another thing altogether. It has a plastic hood which Mrs H places over her head making her look like an employee at a nuclear reactor. The hair dryer bursts into action with a sound like industrial air conditioning.

Although it is a nuisance, I can still hear the TV without turning up the volume much. However, if Mrs H has become interested in the programme, she cranks the sound up so she can hear above what, to her, must seem like being stuck inside a vacuum cleaner.

The fortress walls shake under the impact of the distorted sound. This lasts for about 15 minutes before the cursing resumes as more skin puncturing takes place when the darts are removed from their rollers. Up to two days later, these lethal weapons are still causing havoc as the owners of unsuspecting posteriors leap from the sofa in agony with brightly coloured plastic needles embedded in their bottoms.

I suppose I should be grateful really. I can still remember those early days when Mrs H first became my keeper. She had long straight hair then which seemed to take an age to dry. She used a hand-held dryer and recruited me, her new adoring husband, to help. She would sit on the floor with me on a chair behind her aiming the dryer.

I soon became bored and, through lack of concentration, I would end up waving the hairdryer around as if I was dosing the room with fly spray. This had one of two effects. Either I would hold the dryer so close that Mrs H received a scorched scalp or a startled cat would leap for safety having been roused by a sudden blast of hot air.

Eventually, Mrs H had her hair cut and I was made redundant. I am only called upon now to offer an opinion when the calculations are taking place to establish when her locks will next need to be washed.

"Do you think my hair looks all right? Will it go another day? If I do it tonight, I'll have to do it again before we go out on Saturday."

Fortress H is littered with shampoos, conditioners, mousses and sprays. Not to mention an evil looking tool used to curl the hair which looks like an electric soldering iron with spikes. Me? I've got a comb. So has Brat Minor – somewhere. He rarely uses it. And he complains bitterly when his mother makes him wash his hair. He should worry. Wait till she has him hanging out the washing.

WHY HOCKEY REMINDS ME OF MONOPOLY

It was half way through a match a couple of weeks before Christmas when I first noticed it. My hockey stick had a crack in it. A swift examination told me the damage was terminal. This is always a traumatic experience. The stick becomes like a favourite armchair. It seems to mould itself to you. It becomes an extension of your arms.

It takes time to make friends with a new one – not to mention the fact that the price has shot up considerably since old faithful was bought. And of course, there are all the usual remarks that accompany a fractured stick.

"That'll be it then. You won't bother buying another one at your age. Good time to retire, eh?" These hurtful jibes serve only to galvanise me into inflicting myself on the game for yet another season.

Being so close to Christmas, I thought there would be no problem in acquiring a new one so I left a trail of subtle hints. I kept turning up all over the house hugging my broken stick, shaking my head sadly and releasing heavy sighs of depression that should have melted the hardest heart. Alas, no obviously shaped package appeared at the foot of the tree.

I suppose I could understand this. It is such a personal thing to buy. As I cannot purchase clothes for Mrs H so I should not expect her to choose a hockey stick for me. Perhaps one of those other packages with my name on would yield a supply of money allocated for the very purpose of investing in a new stick. It was not to be so I braved the sales.

There is no way of telling if a stick is suitable until you actually play with it. The best I could do was a few practice swings and dribbles in the shop. There was limited space available and I do apologise to the people nearby who were trying out some ski wear. My perfectly executed pass to the right wing all but removed someone's ankle. As my team mates will tell you, I can do that well enough on the pitch when there is a ball to aim at let alone doing it when there isn't one in sight.

As I left the shop clutching my new limb, I realised that, for the first time, Mrs H was going to find out exactly how much I had paid for it. She has no idea of the cost of such items as hockey sticks. I get away with it by bursting enthusiastically through the door and exclaiming with great excitement what a tremendous bargain I have acquired.

However, thanks to the cashless way of shopping being thrust upon us, my overspending is now exposed. Previously, I would have shelled out readies for this sort of thing but I have got into the habit of using the wretched debit card.

Ah, I hear you say, why don't you spirit the bank statement away so she doesn't see the transaction? No good I am afraid. Mrs H has long since taken control of Fortress finances thanks to my failure to maintain the cheque stubs accurately.

Every month, she sits down with the bank statement and the cheque book to correct all my mistakes. Twice we have gone into the red through my inability to perform simple sums. I hate that moment when I walk into the room and she is sitting at the table tapping away on the calculator surrounded by payment vouchers.

"I don't know what you've done this time. How on earth can you take £64.28 from £273 and come up with an answer of £309?" Being humbled like this makes me see red. Immediately I abdicate all financial responsibility, refuse to complete cheque stubs and state that henceforth the cheque book will be surrendered to her each time I use it to be brought up-to-date. As usual , Mrs H responds with the equine snort and lectures me on the fact that I cannot expect my children to value their money if I do not show a modicum of responsibility myself.

It is not easy to persuade children to appreciate money. We thought a few games of Monopoly might help them get the feel of it but it just seems to bring out the worst in them. Brat Major is quick to acquire property and assumes the guise of an evil landlord. Brat Minor meanwhile tries to hang on to his cash and usually ends up in jail almost penniless. His sister shows him no mercy when he lands on her hotel-infested Park Lane.

Perhaps it's Monopoly that has given them the idea that every time they pass their father they are entitled to a handout. They must think I am the equivalent of "Go".

HOW I GAVE MY ALL FOR THE TEAM

A week ago last Wednesday I woke up feeling fine. By lunchtime I had a throat like a piece of raw meat. Come 4 p.m. I couldn't hold a conversation without punctuating every sentence with a bout of full-blooded hacking. I arrived home from work in desperate need of a corner in which to curl up and die. Mrs H did offer some sympathy but a woman's work is never done – solely by herself. I was soon pressed into service without so much as a Lemsip.

On Friday I surfaced feeling decidedly croaky and coughed at the very thought of speaking. I left for work having growled to Mrs H that I would call off hockey on Saturday. It wasn't emotional blackmail but when I phoned through to excuse myself, I was told not to worry if I couldn't make it. They would only have ten men if I didn't play but they'd just have to manage. Fool that I am I agreed to see how I felt the following morning.

Saturday dawned and after a lie-in I announced to the inmates of Fortress Haverson that I would be damned if I'd let the team down. I would crawl on to the pitch and give it my all – or what remained of it. I would simply turn up, play the game and come home. No stopping for a beer afterwards. You can tell the condition of the patient because Haverson without his post-match pint is like Mrs H without an opinion.

These brave words were fine at 11 a.m. when the sun was shining and the world was calm. Now, unless you were down a coal mine last Saturday afternoon, you will recall that the heavens vented their wrath on us with gale force winds and driving rain. Mrs H already thinks I am 5 minutes short of a full half because I play these silly games. To set out in hurricane conditions with a heavy cold merely confirmed to her that I am in need of some form of counselling. As I left Fortress H both the rain and wind increased in velocity. By the time I arrived at the ground the weather matched my medical diagnosis. Positively awful.

In spite of the elements the game started. The wind howled with delight and summoned endless clouds that lavished upon us their entire stock of horizontal penetrating rain . Within seconds we were soaked but unbelievably we played on.

I was blinded by the rain on my glasses, rendered deaf by the wind and hands that were numb with cold left me with little or no control over my stick. But my game suffered more than most. My cold had blessed me with a blocked nose so I was gasping for breath through my mouth. This in turn aggravated my sore throat. And my seal-like barking cough made my ribs ache. Just what was I doing there?

I thought there might be a glimmer of hope when the footballers on the adjacent pitch gave up at half time and went home. But no, we hockey players are, apparently, made of sterner stuff and launched into the second half. Towards the end of the game I tripped over someone's feet and executed a perfect Jurgen Klinsman dive. I aquaplaned across the mud and came to rest in a puddle. My misery was complete.

To rub salt into the wound, as the final whistle blew, the sky brightened and the rain eased. I hastened to the car and poured myself in. Hunched over the wheel I drove home feeling like a blancmange that was not quite set. I staggered up the path like a wounded soldier returning from the trenches. Brat Major opened the door.

"Dad, you're soaked," she said as she let me in. That was the extent of the sympathy I was to receive for my heroic sortie. And Brat Minor, whose cub's football match had sensibly been cancelled without a ball being kicked, showed not a spark of interest at his father's brave and noble deed.

"I'll go and have a bath," I husked. I plugged in the kettle in the hope that someone would take the hint and bring me a hot drink as I soaked away the aches and pains? Alas no, after I had scrubbed away the mud, I had to make it myself while Mrs H chastised me further. This time for dumping my soggy gear on the back door mat.

Amazingly, by Sunday I was feeling a whole lot better. Now Mrs H is complaining that she doesn't feel quite right. The cure is simple dear. All you have to do is don shorts and a thin shirt, open the bathroom window as wide as you can and climb into a cold shower. I'll lend you my hockey stick.

MY LUNCH HOUR IS BESET WITH PROBLEMS

I am not a shop lifter. However, if you caught sight of me around the city one lunch hour during the week you may be excused for thinking I was up to no good. My problem was that I had forgotten what I had been sent to buy.

The cause of my strife is that the "could you just get..." list, which hitherto was placed in my cereal bowl to greet me in the morning, has been withdrawn. The communication is now delivered verbally. This is my own fault. The shopping list is briefed the night before, during my winding down period. I have completed all outstanding tasks and have been given clearance to slide between the sheets. The opening of my book acts as some kind of trigger which activates Mrs H's vocal chords.

"When you are in the city tomorrow lunch time could you just get..." I grunt every now and again as the list is reeled off. "Now have you got all that? Will you remember or do I need to leave a note?"

"Yes, yes all right," comes my impatient reply as I try to read my book. Within seconds the items I am supposed to get are forgotten as I divide my brain's reception capabilities between my book and Mrs H who usually ends the day by giving me a round up of the day's news.

So there I was, wandering around the city racking my brains to remember what I was supposed to be buying. Inspiration struck. Nail scissors. I headed for a well known chemists. After three quick circuits of the store and one slower one I gave up the search and asked for directions.

"They're over there with the beauty accessories." Of course I should have guessed. I rushed over to the stand and thrust out a hand but stopped in my tracks. Should I buy the stores own brand for £2.50 or the well known brand for £6.99? Go for the cheapest.

Hang on a minute. Do I want straight scissors or the curved ones? Best contact base for further instructions before I speculate any cash. In the meantime, another item from the list had come to mind. I remembered it because of

Mrs H's description.

"I need some of those woggles for Brat Minor's anorak." After interrogation, I had established she meant spring loaded toggles for the pull chords on an anorak. I set off for the haberdashery department of another well known store. Could I see the wretched toggles? Nothing remotely like them in sight. Huge queue at the till and lunch hour rapidly diminishing so it was home to face the music.

Of course, that night, I forgot to check which design of nail scissors was preferred so before my lunchtime sortie the following day a swift phone call was necessary. I was treated to that endearing equine snort from the other end of the phone. "What ever would we want curved nail scissors for and don't forget the woggles."

I accomplished my mission this time although I did have some concern at being spotted rummaging among the beauty accessories for the second day running. Flushed with success I settled down that night to grab a quick read and listen to Mrs H giving the closing headlines. I am amazed that she can jabber away and slap on the preservatives at the same time. How she avoids using the hand cream to remove the eye make-up I just don't know. Especially as she has had further outbreaks of brainlock.

Mrs H's sister and her husband came for the evening. We were in the middle of an intense debate on the pros and cons of privatisation, when Mrs H suddenly began pontificating on a new remedy she had been given for clearing the sinuses. We stared at each other in utter bewilderment. But she really stunned us a few minutes later.

I was lounging in the armchair, full of food and clutching my beer. I was perfectly relaxed, shoes off, sleeves pushed up to my elbows. Without warning Mrs H suddenly sprang from her seat. Marched past her startled sister and headed menacingly in my direction. I sunk into the chair as she bore down on me.

"I'm sorry," she declared, "I can't stand it any longer." With that she grabbed the sleeves of my sweatshirt and pulled them down to my wrists. "You'll stretch them and make them baggy." With that she turned on her heel and returned to her seat as if nothing had happened.

I put all this down to the wine but a few days later she confirmed that she is just as bad when sober. I walked into the kitchen as she was about to fill the kettle. She was steaming at full throttle across the room towards the sink when she was brought to an abrupt halt. The kettle was still plugged in.

SLEEPOVER? IT'S MORE LIKE PANIC!

Mrs H has two speeds at which she usually operates around Fortress H. Overdrive and warp 9. If she ever exceeds warp 9 we know something is afoot. Last week I became aware that on occasions she was little more than a grey blue as she zoomed around the place at a speed approaching that of light.

Sure enough, she was limbering up for something. It was Brat Major's birthday. Thankfully, long gone are the days of the birthday party. Persuading them all to play The Farmer's in his Den and trying to stop the music at the right point in pass the parcel so the same person didn't get all the hidden chocolate.

And I remember vividly clearing up the aftermath. Collecting those disposable plates with gnawed sausage rolls and half eaten chunks of cake. Grinding crisps into the carpet with every step and stacking together the plastic cups only to benefit from an unexpected shower of Coke thanks to one little angel who hadn't finished his drink.

We had the panic over the party bags, that bag of goodies which helps keep W H Smith in business with all the pencils and rubbers they supply for such occasions. There are a few other bits and pieces included, usually edible. Mrs H always tried to add something a bit different.

For one of Brat Major's early parties she popped a couple of bath balls into each bag. These are the things you put in the bath while the water is running and they gradually dissolve into an oily fragrance.

"I wonder," I remarked casually as we bid the last guest farewell, "if any of the little dears will think those bath balls are sweets." Rarely have I seen Mrs H become absolutely motionless then prove that she can accelerate from nought to warp 9 in a micro second.

She grabbed the phone and rang all the mothers and with a voice bordering on hysteria suggesting that party bags should be searched and their owners frisked in order that all bath balls could be accounted for.

We moved on to other treats such as ten pin bowling and this year, by way of celebration, the dear girl wanted the latest fad, a sleepover. In case you haven't stumbled across this one, it means that friends come to stay the night and the rules are supposed to be relaxed. Curfew is extended and food, most of which is normally forbidden, can be consumed at odd hours without the risk of parental wrath.

Mrs H's increased activity was due to the impending day of the sleepover. The place had to be spick and span. This sort of thing always seems odd to me. Why go to all that trouble when three young ladies are going to undo all the good work? But I know better than to argue.

Mrs H wants everything just so. It's as if the guests are going to turn up with notebooks, survey the place and report back to their parents. "The bedrooms were in an awful state. There were clothes everywhere and it didn't look as though she had dusted for a month. And I shouldn't think they possess a paintbrush judging by the decor."

As the day drew near, the atmosphere grew tense and it wasn't just Mrs H. I strolled in one evening and burst into my rendition of Sailing which I believe I perform far better than that awful Rod Stewart. Brat Major responded as if someone had thrown a switch. "Don't you dare do that when I have my sleepover," she exploded with more than a hint of panic in her voice. "It's so embarrassing."

The thought of being let down in front of her chums obviously worried her. On the eve of the sleepover a list of do's and don'ts appeared on the fridge door.

- Don't sing at all anywhere in the house;
- Don't call me any names;
- Don't tell me off under any circumstances;
- Don't tell my friends off or tell them what to do.

We must be allowed to:

- Go to bed at midnight;
- Have a midnight feast – not including Brat Minor;
- Watch a video – without Brat Minor;
- Have my music turned up as loud as I want.

Judging by the noise from the bedroom, the girls seemed to enjoy themselves. So much so that I thought there must be something in this sleepover idea. Choose your own food, do what you like. My birthday is not so very far away, so I have informed Mrs H that, if she has no surprise plans for me to celebrate another passing year, I too will opt for a sleepover.

Just think, I can have white bread and no Aubergine Bake. And I'll write to Joanna Lumley and ask her to keep the date free in her diary. I wonder if she's game for a midnight feast – or something.

LOOSE TALK AFTER A COUPLE OF PINTS

I have to report that I have lost a sparring partner. Akela has decamped to Wales – but not before having the last word. A few months ago I made one of those rash statements, the sort you usually make after a couple of pints. When morning comes you realise the folly of your loose talk and hope no one will take you up on the offer.

"Any time you're short of an adult helper," I said boldly, "let me know." Each week thereafter I'd turn up to collect Brat Minor, hear a noise like a training school for Millwall supporters and thank my lucky stars my offer hadn't been taken up. Then one night the phone rang.

"You said if we were short of help you'd come along. Well we could do with you for the next couple of weeks." He didn't actually say "Gotcha". He did say that these would be his final two weeks in charge before he moved so I thought I ought to see him off. I asked Brat Minor how he felt about me helping at cubs.

"All right as long as you don't wear anything naf and embarrass me." He's getting as bad as his sister.

Now Akela has left the country, I can reveal he has a candle fetish. The first week he had organised cooking sausages over candles. This involves wrapping a banger tightly in tin foil, balancing it on the tines of a fork and holding it in the flame of the candle. I was allocated a Six to supervise. Brat Minor darted up and cackled gleefully, "You've got the worst Six, hah!" and zoomed off.

I thought I had delivered clear instructions but the hysteria in my voice probably caused the message to become distorted because the first cub stabbed his packaged sausage and began to cook it. He was not supposed to pierce the foil as this allowed the fat to drip out. It did. And promptly caught fire.

Of course, his chums thought this was a hoot and soon all the forks at my table were flaming like torches. I managed to persuade them to extinguish their fires and continue frying. I spent the next few minutes dancing round the table re-lighting candles as over-zealous barbecuing snuffed them out.

Small humans are not blessed with the necessary patience to devote time to such an exercise and it wasn't long before they were becoming desperate to sample the fruits of their labours.

They kept peeling back the foil which by this time had become black, to check progress. More fat dripped out, mingled with the soot on the foil and transferred itself to young fingers. These in turn were cleaned with a swift wipe on their owners' uniforms.

Eventually they could wait no longer. The foil was ripped off and bangers, at various stages of cooking, were consumed along with a certain amount of blackened fat. Thankfully to date there have been no reports of food poisoning.

While the pack finished its meeting I helped clear up. The headquarters lacks one vital commodity. Washing up liquid. I'm just glad Mrs H wasn't there to see the sink after twenty blackened and greasy forks had been through it.

The following week I arrived at HQ to learn that we were going to... guess what? Do more cooking with candles. This time it was pancakes, cooked on inverted tin cans. You must know by now what I am like given any sort of tool to use. Well, a grinning Akela handed me a lethal set of cutters and invited me to hack the sides out of the cans. The purpose of this was to allow oxygen to flow freely when they were placed over his beloved candles. He looked almost disappointed when I had finished and was able to present a full set of fingers.

Probably due to my performance the previous week, he had arranged more helpers and I was able to take more of a back seat. Until it was time to clear up.

"Would you mind washing up?" asked Akela wickedly. Not only were the forks still showing the charred signs of candled bangers they were now encrusted with congealed pancake as well. And in spite of the previous week's experience, no one had thought to bring any washing up liquid.

Akela is now in Wales staying in a caravan. You would think a cub leader would, to coin a phrase, be prepared. But Mrs Akela, who is yet to join him, informs me that he forgot to take his sleeping bag and blankets. Fortunately he managed to find a site that was not only open but also had electricity.

Mind you, power and heat shouldn't be any problem for him. I'll bet he didn't forget his candles.

'WE' HAD SUCH FUN DECORATING

Did you know, we have just decorated the master bedroom? I say we because I overheard Mrs H telling someone. I should point out that I took two days off work and I bought the paint. Guess who almost got a hernia heaving the wardrobes around? Who was it who got emulsion in his hair while painting the ceiling? And, yes, I do believe it was me who spent a jolly half hour each day performing that seemingly interminable job of washing out the paint roller.

There is one area where Mrs H's skills would greatly assist. Having been the victim of some of her pastry, she is perfectly qualified to construct filler for me.

I hate filler. I can never get the proportions right. I tip what I think will be the right amount of powder into a bowl and add a little water. Then a little more and then a little more. Before I know it, the mixture is too runny and I have to add more powder.

Eventually I get the consistency right, having mixed what seems to be enough filler to replaster all the walls. Even so, with a couple of holes left to fill, I run out and have to go through the whole rigmarole again. This time I have a load left over which I flush down Mrs H's sink with the usual recriminations.

I get halfway through painting a wall when I come across a hole that has been filled but not sanded. Gently I rub it down and end up with powdered filler on my new paintwork together with a snow-like covering in the can of emulsion.

I've got one of those tubes of flexible filler, the sort you put in a "gun" and squeeze into hairline cracks. I'm no good with that either. I can't get the wretched stuff to squirt into the crack and stay there. When I come to smooth it off, I succeed only in transferring it to the spatula or my hands.

Invariably, when I lay the machine down, I forget to release the trigger and the useless thing continues to dispense its gunge liberally over the walls, the floor and me.

Overall, I had a couple of peaceful days decorating. The Brats were at their seat of learning, where Mrs H is also employed so she was missing most of the day too. I cranked the volume up on the radio and became immersed in my own thoughts.

It was a good job I was on my own in the house when the odd thing went wrong. Especially when I was sanding the skirting board and crunched an already injured finger into the corner of the woodwork. I went on an impromptu walk about, my right hand wedged under my left armpit and screaming words from a selection that aptly suited the occasion but that I would rather my children didn't hear.

As the family had left Fortress H before I started my labours there was none of the usual nagging. "Have you covered everything properly with cloths? You're not going to do the painting with those trousers on are you?"

If I wanted a break there was nobody shouting at me to take my shoes off before I emerged from the room. I will admit that I dropped a splash or two of paint where I should have had protection. And Mrs H did find one of my better jumpers soaking in water to remove the emulsion.

On the second day I finished before Mrs H and the Brats returned home. I eagerly awaited an inspection of my handiwork. Mrs H breezed in and went upstairs to change. Tension mounted as I waited for her to come down but when she did she made no comment at all. I kept dragging decorating into the conversation but still no gushing eulogy paying tribute to my labours. The evening wore on and eventually I could contain myself no longer.

"Bedroom looks pretty good," I piped up brightly.

"Well, I did think the colour would come up more salmony pink than it has but it matches the duvet cover." Oh thank goodness for that. We couldn't have walls that don't match the duvet cover. Whatever would people think?

"I trust you'll clean my sink. There's paint all over it where you've washed your brushes." I know my efforts don't compare to the Sistine Chapel but I bet Michelangelo was not berated by Mrs M when he slid down the ladder and headed for the sink clutching his Turps.

We have to decorate the kitchen soon and with spring upon us, it won't be long before we are out in the garden.

There used to be a window cleaner who served our road but nobody has seen him for months so Mrs H issued a new directive at the weekend. Guess what? In future, we are going to clean our own.

OF COURSE IT WAS SURE TO BE MY FAULT

Mrs H has reacted with venom to my use of the Royal We last week in connection with my recent solo decorating of the bedroom. She was conspicuous by her absence from any sort of involvement. In reply she issued the following statement which was addressed to all inmates of Fortress Haverson and anyone within earshot of the open window.

"Excuse me. Who booked time off while I was at work and when the children had hair appointments so I couldn't help? And who had time off at half term but wanted to go out for the day instead of painting?" Somehow I thought it would be my fault.

"And it was me who eventually cleaned out the sink where you had made a mess with your brushes," she added pointedly. She went on to list all the places where paint was splashed and accused me of tearing the valance when I shunted the bed around the room.

I fought back lamely by reminding her that she had failed to compliment me on the quality of my workmanship. Perhaps it was being denied the opportunity to contribute to the painting that made her feel guilty and thus unable to praise me.

Besides, she likes getting compliments. She couldn't wait to tell me the flattering remark that bus driver made to her the other day. Mind you, having heard what he said, I don't think he's fit to be behind the wheel.

Mrs H was getting out of the car at the Park and Ride. This is an operation in itself. She is the only person I know who can go on a shopping expedition with her bag half full before she starts.

It contains an umbrella, gloves, and an assortment of carrier bags to cope with the overspill resulting from her overspending. There's a wodge of tissues, a magazine to read when she stops for coffee and I even found a toothbrush in there the other day.

Anyway, she was in the process of checking that everything was intact and the car locked when the bus came into view. She was some distance from the pick-up point but the bus stopped beside the car and waited for her to climb on board.

She thanked the driver for his consideration. His reply demonstrated that his eyesight is such that he should not be in charge of a vehicle.

"That's all right," he said. "I'll do anything for a good looking woman." What? I demand he be tested. He should not be allowed on the road. This bit of flattery made Mrs H's day and she became most irritable when predictably I came out with all the obvious comments.

"Did you help him search for his contact lenses?"

I backed off when she accused me of spoiling things for her. We were lurching dangerously towards " You never say nice things to me."

I can't get away with comments like the bus driver made. I told Mrs H of a recent incident when I was going to compliment a lady. This particular girl was wearing a rather nice perfume. I was about to tell her so when I bottled out in case I was accused of trundling out a hackneyed old chat-up line. To my surprise, Mrs H offered me guidance.

"Huh, she snorted, "All you had to say was something like 'That's a nice perfume you are wearing. What is it called? I would like to buy my wife some for her birthday.'"

This filled me with suspicion. Mrs H has never coached me in handling other women before. Maybe she was just angling for some perfume. Or has she had enough and was preparing me for a new owner?

Actually, I would like to pay a compliment to Mrs H; for her selection of carpet for the bedroom. I'd like to – but she hasn't chosen it yet. She claims she hasn't had time to look for one. I can see what will happen. The bedroom will need decorating again before she gets round to it.

Oh my, the rigours of running Fortress Haverson. What a drain on her time the Brats and I must be – and we never tell her how much we appreciate her. Perhaps I should try another approach. Suppose I opt out and become grant maintained. I could set myself up as a Trust, have my own budget and simply buy in Mrs H's services.

If the meals don't come up to scratch, I can withhold payment and put the supply of future Aubergine Bakes out to tender. I shall expect provisions to be readily available. Not how it is at present. My healthy bowl of muesli has been missing these past few mornings because you know who failed to replenish the stocks when she went shopping.

I suppose this is the equivalent of privatising Mrs H. Ah but that means there is a danger she might find a higher bidder than me.

Hmm, perhaps I better find out the name of that perfume after all.

NORMALITY STARTS AND ENDS WITH ME

Help. If you see me in public behaving strangely, please let me know. I am clinging to my status as the only resident at Fortress Haverson that's normal. I should hate the quirks of the other inmates to rub off on me.

Brat Minor's grey matter continues to let him down. If we ask him to do something, we have to sit on him to make sure he does it straight away. If he is given time to allow other thoughts to gain access to his mind, the original instruction becomes so diluted that it is lost in dreams of scoring last minute winning goals and slaying aliens.

Last weekend, Brat Major announced that her dozy brother had not eaten breakfast. "Don't let me catch you eating during the morning." I warned. "Your mother will not be pleased if she cooks lunch and you turn your nose up at it."

Brat Minor took exception to this and insisted that he had eaten a hearty breakfast of Rice Krispies. Brat Major pointed out that there were only two cereal bowls waiting for her father to wash up. One was hers and one was her mothers.

"If you had breakfast, which bowl did you use?" I demanded

"The blue one." he replied indignantly. Said bowl was still in the cupboard.

"Well, Mum must have washed it up and put it away." The chances of Mrs H washing up the breakfast things when I am at home are about as slim as Joanna Lumley coming to my birthday sleepover.

In fact the breakfast that was "on screen" in his mind was the previous day's. His memory of it was obviously so vivid that it satisfied his appetite a whole 24 hours later.

The other evening he was sent to get ready for bed. Five minutes later he reappeared. The only visible difference was that he was clutching a glass of apple juice. What else he had been doing during his absence we never did find out.

It gets worse. Last Sunday, Mrs H spotted what looked like a raffia mat on his head and immediately prescribed a hairwash. An hour or so later he was just off to bed when she casually said, "You did wash your hair didn't you?" There was a look as blank as our bank account when Mrs H has been let loose with the cheque book. He simply couldn't remember whether he'd done it or not.

And then there is the loquacious Mrs H. She who never uses two words where twenty will do. Since I mentioned a couple of times recently her capacity to talk., I have heard her, on more than one occasion, offering a reason for her verbosity. Only a woman could come out with this explanation. In fact, probably only Mrs H could.

She claims she has such a limited vocabulary that she has to use lots of words to get her message across. That sounds like a contradiction in terms. In fact, what she does is to supply all the background information that surrounds the plot. When Mrs H tells a story, it's rather like heading for the motor way but opting for the scenic route only to find there is a diversion via the country lanes.

She was on the phone the other night, telling someone what she had been up to the previous afternoon. To get to the point of her story, she detailed the diary of the entire family for that day in a dramatic and protracted build-up.

"Neil had the day off to look after the children. Brat Minor went ten pin bowling at a friends birthday party. We took them bowling for their parties last year. Of course I didn't do it, you wouldn't catch me making a fool of myself. Anyway because he had the party, Brat Major went shopping with her father...oh that reminds me I'm looking for a pair of flat shoes to go with that new skirt..." And we were paying for the call.

Brat Major remains relatively sane but extremely truculent. If this is what she is like at the age of twelve, the teenage years are going to be like World War 3. It is rare for us to exchange a civil word with her these days. She displays a bravado as if nothing matters.

"You'll get into trouble if you don't do your homework."

"So? I don't care. It doesn't matter. Lots of people don't finish their homework." All this is said with the head inclined slightly back so the retort is fired at you down her nose. At the same time her face and eyes generate messages of distaste and contempt.

Thank goodness I am there to bring reason and common sense to prevail on the household. The only trouble is, no one ever listens to me.

WHO ELSE COULD BE OUR RUDDER?

Mrs H has been so busy recently that I and the young inmates have gained an insight into what life at Fortress Haverson might be like if we were ever left to fend for ourselves. Things were so hectic for her that some of her domestic activities were neglected.

She whinged all last weekend about how much she had to do. How she was way behind with the housework, the freezer was almost empty and, in spite of a blitz on it, the ironing pile seemed as bottomless as Brat Minor's money box.

She then proceeded to vanish for the best part of three days. Appearing at Fortress Haverson to provide the odd meal, demonstrate her skill at the art of delegation and grab a few hours kip. What with her part-time job, various meetings, shopping and a trip to London it was Thursday before she was stationary for sufficient time for me to ask for some pocket money.

It's all very well her gallivanting about but a chap could get complacent. I am used to being driven ever onward. Suddenly Fortress H was rudderless and I found myself making decisions that are usually way above my station. "Can I have a Coke with my tea?" which was usually supported by the bluff, " Mum always lets me."

I have come up with a solution to maintain continuity and discipline. I will advertise for a locum. A kind of surrogate nag. Watch the employment columns in the EDP for my advertisement.

"Person required to deputise for often absent wife/mother. Full board in exchange for the few light duties carried out by the regular incumbent. Job entails providing minimal services for amiable, anxious to please father and two bolshy Brats. Meals are expected but not time-critical. Residents are used to them being served as and when ready.

"Vacuum cleaner provided. Low mileage, one careful lady owner. Sewing appreciated but no pressure other than a request that the garments are repaired before they go out of fashion.

"No gardening, decorating or washing up. Faithful old retainer performs all these duties and is on call at anytime to provide labour or spider removal. No need to worry if he's watching TV.

"Children easy to deal with. The only qualification required is the ability to stand at the bottom of the stairs and shout. Care must be taken here as Faithful Old Retainer is so well trained he too responds to bellowed orders.

"No alarm clock required. Faithful old retainer sounds reveille and offers snooze facility. In fact no time-piece needed as household ceased to operate in accordance with Greenwich Mean Time several years ago.

"Applicants should be of determined nature. Long periods of silences are not familiar so they must be able to talk at length without pausing for breath. They should also have a grasp of a wide range of subjects. The residents are used to a constant supply of freely dispensed advice on all topics.

"Laundry service essential. Brats can mess up an entire wardrobe in 24 hours They will expect the clothes ready to wear the next day and senior resident is incapable of operating the washing machine. Service for hanging out washing is provided but clear instructions on what to peg where will be expected.

"Candidates must be able to spend money as if it is liberally provided by Mother Nature.

"Applications to Fortress Haverson in a plain brown envelope marked 'Doddle'"

I know we couldn't manage without her and as someone said to me the other day: "She can't be that bad. You've been together a long while."

"I suppose I've got used to her," I replied generously, knowing she is irreplaceable.

"You mean she's like a favourite pair of socks that you just can't throw away?" Perhaps there is some truth in that. Do I see Mrs H as that baggy old jumper that I refuse to let go to a jumble sale? The one I like to slop around the house in, wear for gardening but wouldn't dream of being seen wearing it in public. I asked Mrs H if she thought that was a fair summary of our marriage.

"Huh," she snorted. "You mean you see me as a comfy old pair of carpet slippers." She was rinsing some washing in the sink as she contemplated her response. I thought the ferocity with which she was plunging the clothes into the water quite unnecessary. "I'd like to think there's more than just familiarity there. A bit of spark somewhere." The clothes were subjected to another severe ducking and I backed off.

Things were beginning to sound rather ominous. I think I'd better keep an eye on the situation vacant columns. Perhaps you'll let me know if you see an advertisement that reads something like, "Faithful Old Retainer required. Must have a bit of a spark."

THERE ARE NICE THINGS ABOUT MRS H

I'm in trouble again. Mrs H read last week's column where I floated the idea of advertising for someone to deputise in her absence. At first she showed signs of pleasure but as she read on she was unimpressed with the job profile which, for some reason, she assumed was modelled on her.

Even my comment that she is irreplaceable failed to have the desired mellowing effect. "I thought you were going to break the habit of a lifetime and say something nice about me," she complained.

She responded with spirit to my closing remarks that she might retaliate by advertising for a Faithful Old Retainer to replace me. "If I put an advert in, it would be for a Faithful Young Retainer." Ouch! No whipper-snapper would put up with what I have to.

I'd like to see her give her toyboy the grillpan after she's been cooking bacon. Let him try and get it clean. And this young Chippendale will need broad shoulders to handle the criticism that his best endeavours will attract when he tries to help around the house.

Take the bathroom. Simple job to clean it wouldn't you say? A couple of squirts of Jif and a bit of elbow grease. Not if I do it – apparently. I make sure there is a good whiff of disinfectant around so she'll think I am doing a thorough job but there is this lack of trust in my ability.

"You did that rather quickly. Did you take everything off the window sill or just wipe round them? Look at the taps. You never do the taps properly." Who cares about the taps? No sooner do I walk out of the bathroom than the younger inmates zoom in having been ordered to wash their hands. Hands that have been in places I'd rather not know about.

Her young hero will have to be pretty good at such complicated operations as changing the sheets. Another job I can't get right. I don't "plump up" her pillow. I don't pull the bottom sheet tight enough. There are creases in it. "Did you give the duvet a good shake? All the filling is at the bottom. I can't wrap it round me and keep warm."

Then the words that ought to be music to my ears; "I'd rather do it myself if you are not going to do it properly." Fine. Get on with it. The trouble is, she doesn't leave it there. She rattles off all the other jobs she has to do before she climbs into that uncomfortable bed. She has this knack of leaving me riddled with guilt when she delivers her payoff line.

"You'll have to tape the film, I won't be finished in time to see it." This always makes me see red. Probably because I want to see the film and I know, and she knows, that I couldn't sit there for a couple of hours glued to the box while she is grafting.

There follows a sharp exchange. I try to ascertain why she has to iron Brat Major's jeans before midnight and she grabs the opportunity to give me a preview of all the jobs she has in store for the following night. By the time we have called a truce, we've missed the start of the film anyway.

I must admit I do have a twinge of conscience. Particularly as last weekend was our 22nd wedding anniversary. It does beg the question that if my life is so awful, how come we are on the way to negotiating our third decade together?

I would like, therefore, to take the opportunity to pay tribute to the human dynamo that powers me and the young inmates to such high achievements, Mrs H. This woman who, only the other night as I was heading for bed just after midnight, was still at it, hanging washing on the clothes horse. The wife that always adds to that shopping list a supply of beer for her husband.

The lady who mothered our children. Two little mavericks who treat me like Barings Bank; using my resources to invest in all sorts of projects with the promise of high returns but which only yield requests for further loans.

If it wasn't for her I wouldn't have clean shirts with colour co-ordinated ties. The Aubergine Bake would have passed me by and my digestive system would still be in the slow lane thanks to white bread.

Mrs H reaches further than just her family. To our neighbours, her voice is the first sign of summer. For some this is the sound of the Cuckoo but when you stand outside and can hear Mrs H bellowing at the Brats, the windows of Fortress Haverson must be open. The weather is getting warmer.

There, I bet she wouldn't get a eulogy like that from any faithful young retainer.

I'M STITCHED UP FOR WINTER

Mrs H put down her magazine. She looked up with a self-satisfied smile and addressed me with those words that generally herald some form of put down.

"I hate to tell you this," she announced, "but Rod Stewart seems a really nice person." What? Him with the voice that sounds like the noise of a Black and Decker test laboratory?

"And according to this article," she persisted, "He had the top album and single in both the American and British charts at the same time. Elvis didn't even manage that." Wow! there's something to tell the grandchildren as you bounce them on your knee. I must admit, at the mere mention of his name my interest had waned instantly but Mrs H was not to be put off.

"Are you listening to me Neil Haverson?" she rasped. "The Times reckons he has one of the best voices ever to sing in a rock band." That doesn't say much for the rest of them – or The Times for that matter. Anyway, I am sure our Rod achieves his drone thanks solely to those crippling tight trousers he wears. I'm surprised his blood ever gains entry to the lower torso.

"Anybody can be made to sound good in an article," I protested. "Why, I even make you sound good in mine." As soon as I said it I regretted it.

You see, she is still banging on about the manner in which she has been portrayed in my previous couple of columns. I thought I had laid this to rest last week with my moving tribute to the quality of life she has created at Fortress Haverson. Apparently not. My ill-advised remark, forced out of me by discussing that awful Rod Stewart, opened up the old wound.

"You made me sound like a housekeeper and mother. Nothing more," she complained. "What about that extra bit of spark? I must be all right if we've been married this long." Then she really stunned me. "And you didn't even mention my body." It is comments out of the blue like this which lead me to question the whereabouts of her marbles. But she was on a roll now.

"I'm proud of the way I've changed my body. I work hard to keep my body in shape." Perhaps she should bring out a keep fit video. "Banish those Jodhpur Thighs with

Mrs H ." She could get Rod Stewart to introduce it. Oh no, he only likes blonds. Mental note; check bathroom cabinet for peroxide.

It is difficult to keep pace with her thought processes sometimes. A recent example was Good Friday. I was out in the garden when I became aware of a gentle whirring sound emanating from Fortress H. Puzzled, I went into the house to find the source. Was it Brat Minor performing one of his experiments with electricity? Was he trying to wire his sister to the mains? Much worse. Mrs H had the sewing machine out.

There was a short burst of whirring followed by a heartfelt curse. More whirring, more cursing then a triumphant "Hah!" as if she had just succeeded in splitting the atom. I decided it was best to keep a low profile until she had finished.

Eventually she appeared before me with a huge grin on her face. "Don't get excited," she said proudly, "but I've mended your old anorak." My hopes soared. At last, that anorak with the torn pockets that had been booked in for repairs some two and half years ago was wearable again.

Wrong again. Mrs H produced a paint stained garment which I thought had long since been consigned to a jumble sale. Goodness knows how long she'd had it stashed away but its once torn zip was now neatly stitched. "It's the one you wear in the winter for gardening," she said, her voice oozing with pleasure. I thought carefully about this. It was a cracking day, sunny and warm. Temperatures had reached 17 degrees, high for the time of year. I conveyed my conclusion to her very slowly.

"So you've been locked away, slaving over your sewing machine, just as winter has ended, to repair an anorak which I can wear in the winter." Yes, I suppose this was a little lacking in appreciation of her efforts but the logic somehow escaped me.

I suppose it could have been worse. She might have had a pair of my trousers on her sewing machine. Making them tighter to give me a voice like her ageing pop star hero. Come to think of it, she does keep saying there must be a spark somewhere that has kept us together so long. Perhaps this is the very thing that could cause combustion.

Maybe I better get the peroxide.

TECHNOLOGY IS GIVING ME NIGHTMARES

As usual, the approach of lunchtime heralded the arrival of dark clouds. Although I had no coat or umbrella Mrs H wanted me to spend some money so out I had to go. I left the office with a fellow slave and, as we hastened about our business, I confided that I was troubled with more than just the weather.

"I'm on a mission for Mrs H." I explained to her. "I am supposed to buy something but I can't remember what it is." Yes, there had been a reminder awaiting me at breakfast, carefully placed in my cereal bowl. Unfortunately I had removed the note for the not unreasonable purpose of pouring a healthy portion of muesli into it.

"I'm going to head for the shops and hope something strikes a chord when I get there," I added without too much hope. This spawned some discussion on how I might find a way of jogging my memory.

"What you want is one of those Dictaphones," said my colleague. What a frightening thought. I can see myself steaming into Marks and Spencers, clutching my machine, guided by a recorded Mrs H. It would be like a treasure hunt.

"Go up the first escalator and turn right at the jeans. Carry on past the shirts, right at the socks and the trousers I saw are right in front of you."

I wonder if people would stare. They probably would if the store had done what they tend to do periodically which is to shuffle all the display stands. Where the suits were on Saturday, you find the underwear on Monday. There I'd stand, in a state of total confusion, with Mrs H burbling away in my right hand.

Imagine walking around the Supermarket with a speaking shopping list. I suppose I could actually play it to the assistant on the delicatessen counter. I couldn't be accused of buying the wrong meat then.

"I want a quarter of a pound of ham. Don't let them give you that thick sliced fatty stuff. Oh and while you're there get a pound of mature cheddar. Not the one that smells like Brat Minor's bedroom."

The possibilities go beyond shopping lists. Mrs H could exert her influences over me all day long. Perhaps she'd treat me to a tape of heavy breathing. No, more likely corrective phrases or words of motivation for me to play if my morale slipped. For example, when I walk past the vending machine and fancy a cheese and pickle roll, I could kill off my appetite by playing the moving statement she issued the other evening when I returned home with a new pair of trousers.

"If you're short, fat and wide, you can't expect to look right in trousers with pleats."

Of course I'd have to go somewhere private to get my fix of Mrs H's rousing comments. I wouldn't want the rest of the office to hear me being urged to "make sure you eat that yoghurt I gave you."

Daily orders could be taped for me. Just think what a time saver that would be. As I drive home I could listen to my instructions for the evening. Tape A for fine weather and outside jobs. Tape B for when it's wet. The following morning, on my journey into work, I could listen to a debrief on how I performed the previous evenings tasks.

"The cupboard door in the kitchen is still coming off the hinge. Buy a new hinge in the city today. Details of size of hinge are given later on the tape. You left your screw driver on the kitchen floor. Brat Minor fell over it and cut his knee. And don't be late home for tea tonight. We're having Aubergine Bake."

I suppose, as technology becomes more sophisticated, I could find myself equipped with a mini TV camera linked via satellite to Fortress Haverson. Mrs H in the control room could navigate me to the exact shelf to buy a shirt.

"Keep going, keep going, next shelf up. No, not the orange ones, the blue ones on the left. Are you listening to me? Stop looking at that girl with the short skirt."

This brings a whole new meaning to home shopping. From her bunker, Mrs H could direct me around the city and do her window shopping from the armchair. That could be embarrassing if she spots something in Dorothy Perkins she wants a good look at. I would be left with my nose pressed against the glass staring intently at a nice little off the shoulder number.

There would be no escape. Or would there? Just think, with this electronic wizardry, I could do something I've never been able to do before. When Mrs H is in full rabbit, I could pull the plug.

MANY HANDS SPOIL THE BROTH

I am sure it must have been a woman who dreamed up many of our well known sayings. Just think about it. So many of them contradict each other. For example, "Look before you leap" conflicts with "He who hesitates is lost."

As further proof, I offer as evidence, the chain of events at a recent Sunday lunch when the head of Fortress catering – yes Mrs H – started off with the maxim "Many hands make light work" but ended up proving that "Too many cooks spoil the broth".

All inmates were summoned to help with dinner. I was assigned the potatoes to scrub, Brat Major was allocated the carrots to slice and Brat Minor was instructed to set the table. Mrs H was like a foreman, moving among us chivvying us along. We all failed miserably. First she had a go at me.

"Have you got all the grot off the potatoes? Yuk! Just look at all those black bits. That's soil – and we'll be crunching our way through it." Then she turned her attention to the efforts of the junior catering assistants.

"You haven't sliced the carrots thinly enough. They'll take ages to cook." she informed Brat Major who, I thought, just for a moment, wielded the kitchen knife with undue menace.

"Aren't we having a sweet?" Mrs H inquired with heavy sarcasm of Brat Minor. He looked at her with utter bewilderment. "You haven't put any dessert spoons out," his mother explained.

At this point the younger inmates exercised their rights as children to ignore anything a parent tells them to do if it doesn't suit them. They downed tools and left the kitchen grizzling that when they did help all they got was criticism.

I know better than to attempt mutiny so I kept my head down. As I expected, Mrs H let fly a short sharp vocal blast and the pair of them returned sullenly to the kitchen. Both were extremely irritable at being pressed back into service so they embarked on a campaign of dissent.

Brat Major attacked the carrots with the knife as if she was severing limbs. Meanwhile, Brat Minor grudgingly extracted the dessert spoons from the draw and flung them at random on the table. Then, when he needed an additional chair, he demonstrated that endearing feature of his where he shows a total absence of common sense.

The spare chair was on the opposite side of the table to the space. All he had to do was shuffle the chairs round a place and add the extra one. Instead he grabbed the spare chair and, threatening paintwork, furniture and the physical safety of his sister lurched all the way round the table with it like a drunken weight lifter.

By now they were both in a thoroughly bad mood and decided a bit of sibling rivalry would help make their point. An argument broke out as to who was to sit where.

"I want to sit next to Dad," announced Brat Minor and moved my place setting.

"No you're not, it's my turn," protested Brat Major making a dive for the cutlery. Before we knew it they were locked in a full scale tug of war with the table cloth and Brat Minor's already shambolic table plan had been completely wrecked.

Eventually a compromise was struck. They agreed to sit beside each other with me opposite. Now they could both share in the uplifting experience of watching me eat.

Finally the meal was ready to be served. Most of Mrs H's food is unacceptable to them and attracts the description of "gross". Each portion was greeted with disbelief that they could be expected to eat it.

"Don't give me many peas. I hate peas," claimed one while the other announced, "If you give me all those potatoes, I shan't eat them."

The head of catering was getting extremely ragged. Having spent some considerable time creating a tasty sauce in which to serve the chicken she was not amused at the upturned pair of noses that greeted her culinary efforts. But the discontent continued unabated.

"Oh no, there's mushrooms in it. I hate mushrooms." That was it. While I would have "let sleeping dogs lie", Mrs H decided to "strike while the iron was hot". Either they accepted gratefully what was placed before them or they went without.

For once, I would have been right as all the moaning was for nothing. Brat Major, being such a devotee of food, Hoovered everything that was put in front of her. While Brat Minor is so absent minded, he forgot his loathing of mushrooms and ate the lot without complaint.

Now, you may think that "he who pays the piper calls the tune" so I should have taken charge of this whole episode. But I know one proverb it's better not to contradict. "Don't bite the hand that feeds you."

TALKING TURKEY AT FORTRESS H

One of my major roles at Fortress Haverson is that of co-defendant. If either of the younger inmates is in the dock being cross examined by Mrs H, I find I'm in there with them.

I was on a joint charge a couple of weekends ago, though I must admit that, to start with, it was my fault. We were going out and Mrs H wanted to prepare a Sunday lunch that she could quickly reheat. She suggested either a chicken pie or shepherd's pie.

"I've got some mince but if you want chicken, you'll have to go and buy it," she announced. No contest. With indecent haste, we voted for chicken. Let me say here, there is nothing wrong with Mrs H's shepherd's pie. Relatives and friends have dined on it and all made full recoveries.

Brat Minor accompanied me to the butchers but we arrived just as he had sold the last chicken. The butcher offered, instead, a boned turkey joint. Imagine my dilemma. Return without a chicken and condemn us all to shepherd's pie. Or take something for which I had not been given buying authority. I knew whichever I did would be wrong.

I turned to Brat Minor for support but he has already learnt that it is best to stay neutral when decisions have to be made. Then a vista of the shepherd's pie manifested itself before me and I plumped for the turkey. I asked the butcher for a note to take home explaining my predicament but he politely declined saying that, under the circumstances, he would probably close as soon as we had left.

We arrived at Fortress H and I thrust the turkey joint into Brat Minor's arms. "You can give it to your mother." He took a few brave steps in the direction of the back door before he suffered an outbreak of cowardice and flung the joint back at me. We continued down the path tossing the meat between us like a couple of Will Carlings.

The joint was with me when we reached the door. Purposefully, I stepped inside but before I could open my mouth a grinning Brat Minor forced his way through and cackled in delight: "Dad's got something to tell you. They didn't have a chicken so he bought this dirty great turkey joint."

Having delivered this loyal outburst he disappeared leaving me to face the music. Mrs H proceeded to question me closely on the transaction. Her relative calm was shattered when my answer to "How much did it cost?" sank in.

"What? £8! I only wanted a chicken to make a pie. You know I haven't got time to do a proper roast." She then launched into a passionate speech which centred around the absence of any power of rational thought I may once have possessed. This was followed by her usual response when her time is put under pressure. I was subjected to a run down of her entire workload for the next two days.

I retired to the garden to cut the hedge. While I was hacking away, it transpired that I wasn't the only one doing some trimming. Brat Major was in her bedroom with a friend from a neighbouring house. Unbeknown to us a bit of amateur crimping was being practised. To my absolute horror, I discovered that our daughter had got carried away with the scissors and chopped her mate's fringe.

Both girls were consumed with panic as to what parental wrath might be unleashed upon them. I led a trembling Brat Major next door to apologise but neither of us had the courage to tell Mrs H. Brat Major made the decision for me by making a dash to her room where she remained for the next couple of hours.

For the second time that day Mrs H went ballistic. Now, this is the type of situation where I share the blame for other people's offences. By the time Mrs H had finished berating me and the absent Brat Major, I was convinced that it was I who had wielded the scissors. What made it worse, was that any other offence I had committed in the past month was taken into consideration. Needless to say, the incident involving the turkey joint was dredged up again and the "trial" was rounded off with a harassed Mrs H giving a further run down of all her outstanding jobs.

Things had calmed down by the next day. The turkey was devoured without complaint. In fact it was hardly mentioned. Instead, the lunchtime conversation turned to a planned trip to London.

"Do you know," said Mrs H "It costs £7.95 for an adult to get into the Tower of London?" I couldn't resist it. I turned to Brat Minor.

"Do you know," I informed him. "You can buy a turkey joint for what it costs to get into the Tower of London?"

YOU NEVER KNOW WHAT WILL COME OUT IN THE WASH

The Fortress laundry seems to operate 24 hours a day. No sooner is one load done than Mrs H is rallying us to the cause with her cry of "Anything for a blue wash? Jeans inside out, zips up. Don't forget to empty your pockets." That last instruction is lost on the amnesiac Brat Minor. Only last week his key ring, badge and plastic library card had the benefit of a hot wash followed by a rinse and spin.

Although Mrs H found it rather amusing, she ought to know by now that his memory is about as effective as my argument that someone else should do the washing up. She should check his pockets before his trousers are treated to the relief of a much needed union with something biological.

Since then a battery and a pair of nail clippers have also enjoyed a wallow in detergent. And the final horror, for Brat Minor anyway, was that he forgot to take his treasured Premiership football cards from his shirt pocket so they all received an early bath.

Brat Minor's main problem is lack of concentration. He told us such a woeful tale of how he found himself in trouble at school because he hadn't listened properly. The teacher had told the class to get out their books for the next part of the lesson. Brat Minor complied but some of his chums did not. As a result, the teacher issued the following invitation to them.

"All those who haven't got their books out, STAND UP!" Brat Minor, having carried out the original order, had drifted off. Unfortunately for him, he rejoined the proceedings just as the teacher belted out the "STAND UP!" instruction.

Obediently, our hapless hero sprung to his feet only to discover that those who had stood up would be missing break for not doing as they had been told. His bitter complaint at suffering what he considered to be a gross miscarriage of justice was dismissed by Mrs H on the grounds that it was his own fault for not paying attention.

Mrs H really is a case of the pot calling the kettle black. This is the woman who, the other evening, prepared for my tea something novel with courgettes. Proudly, she served up the meal and I seized my knife and fork. I did have this feeling that something was missing but I know better than to ask questions. I was about to dig in when she let out a shriek.

"I've forgotten the sauce!" Since it formed an integral part of the meal, it is hard to see how she could have overlooked it but there it was, still bubbling away on the cooker. It gets worse.

I returned home one evening after working late to find that Mrs H had taken the children to a school disco and was staying to help. Of course, this doesn't mean a free evening for yours truly and sure enough, waiting for me on the kitchen work surface was a list.

"Neil" it said in large letters at the top. Somehow, she even writes my name with authority. It seemed to leap out of the paper at me. "Get washing off line." Dutifully I headed to the washing line. Nothing. Absolutely nothing. Aha, I wondered, had she used the tumble dryer but no, this too was empty.

On her arrival home, I informed her that I had spent some considerable time searching the garden for non-existent washing. Her reply made me shake my head sadly in despair. She confessed that not only had she got the washing in herself but she had written the note for me after she had done it.

I should also mention that among the other orders on the list was an item which said, "I don't mind what you tape on television tonight." At first glance that may sound generous. However, if you think a bit deeper, you will realise that this simple sentence contains a pointed warning. "Don't think you can get away with watching television because I am not here. Tape it."

I know I am forgetful too but one advantage of being a mere foot soldier at Fortress Haverson is that I don't have to remember anything. There is always something or someone there to jog my memory. Be it one of Mrs H's lists or a pestering Brat who requires one of the few unskilled services I am able to offer. Usually the supply of money.

If Mrs H has nagged me to the point where she thinks further sniping will prove counter productive, she tries to be cunning. She communicates through a Brat.

"Perhaps you can persuade your father to put the suitcases in the loft before someone falls over them and breaks a leg."

At least, if I forget to do something, Mrs H can't make me miss my break. I don't get one.

THE PAIN IN MRS H'S LIFE WASN'T ME

For most of the year I am a pain in the back to Mrs H. Last Saturday, the pain was there in her back but it wasn't me. Somehow, in the never ending struggle to place Fortress H at the forefront of domestic culture, she had done some damage. Come Saturday morning the poor old thing was in such a sad way, she was reduced to asking me to tie her shoe laces. By the afternoon she could barely walk.

Usually, Mrs H sits down only to eat or for a few minutes before she goes to bed. She rarely sits and watches television without doing something else such as ironing. But there she was able to move with only the greatest of effort and a substantial amount of pain.

Sunday you will recall was Fathers Day and Mrs H was catering for all fathers and their sons and daughters. Panic was setting in. But when the chips are down who has she got waiting in the wings?

"There's the cooking... ouch... to do. And the housework. I'll never get it... owwwhh... done," she wailed. Fear not. The faithful old retainer and the young inmates were there to save the day. I was promoted to deputy supervisor. As Mrs H staggered upstairs to lie on the bed, I rallied my workforce.

Brat Major disappeared to the kitchen to cook. Brat Minor and I volunteered for the housework and staged our first assault on the north wing. We produced a Herculean effort. It was a good job Mrs H couldn't see her son renovating her china. He attacked it with his duster as if he was trying to clean dead flies off a car windscreen.

I wound up the Hi Fi and, with Whitney Houston belting out the theme from The Bodyguard, the adrenaline flowed. I put the vacuum cleaner through manoeuvres yet to be included in the handbook.

But from her sick bed, Mrs H was keeping tabs on us. If we were going to do it, it had to be done properly. Unfortunately, we got our timings wrong. She sent an emissary to us in the form of Brat Major.

"Mum says you can't possibly be vacuuming yet. You have to dust everything first and brush the upholstery or there's no point in vacuuming." I thought of about three messages to send back but better judgement prevailed. One day soon Mrs H would be fit again.

Finally, Mrs H's natural desire to organise outweighed the pain. She lurched downstairs to check on us. Fortunately she got side-tracked in the kitchen with her daughter.

By now I was working solo. My young helper had soon lost interest and, taking advantage of his mother's lack of mobility, had made himself scarce. I wasn't so lucky. She spotted me and moved me on to the next task.

"Bathroom and toilet next. Do the toilet first, use the blue cloth. Use the old sponge for the bath and sink." She delivered my orders, yelped with pain and hobbled off. Armed with a good supply of Jif and disinfectant I began cleaning. Foolishly, I became immersed in my thoughts and dropped my guard. I failed to notice Mrs H stagger up for a spot inspection.

"You're using my best sponge! And make sure you shine the taps properly." Another groan and she went back to supervising the cooking. My final chore was to sweep the stairs then dust and vacuum the hall. No problem. I was well down the stairs when a pain-wracked voice husked a message.

"It takes me ten minutes to do the stairs properly." I was way ahead. I had a mere four stairs to go and had been at it for less than half the time. They looked perfectly okay to me. Whatever does she do? No wonder she takes so long to do the housework.

Next morning, the pain in Mrs H's back had eased slightly. Although still in some agony, she took over the reins of Fortress management and my temporary secondment to deputy supervisor was ended. I was regraded to gardener/labourer.

Mrs H turned in a magnificent effort, firing on all cylinders despite the constant pain. In the end, she was ahead of schedule. This must have been due in some small way to the outstanding performance of the previous day carried out under the guidance of the temporary deputy supervisor,

The rest of the family arrived and went into shock at finding her in an armchair reading the Sunday paper. They reacted like a Twitcher who has spotted a species of bird he thought was extinct.

Mrs H had one regret from her enforced period of inactivity. "It's no good, I shouldn't sit around. Just look at my nails. I've bitten them right down because I didn't have anything to do."

Somehow, I don't seem to have that problem.

THERE IS ALWAYS SOMETHING NEW TO LEARN

Be fair. I have never been backward in coming forward about my shortcomings when it comes to all things practical. Mrs H knows this but does not spare a chap's sensitivities when an opportunity arises to remind me of my inadequacies.

Her latest dig came as we were discussing the bathroom. The suite is in grave need of replacing but unfortunately there is nothing in the Fortress refurbishing budget to pay for it. I was suggesting ways around the problem.

"If we buy the suite and find a plumber to install it perhaps..." That was as far as I got. Mrs H's response was instant.

"If you're doing the tiling, I'm leaving home. I can't cope with that. I remember the last time you attempted it." Thank you for your support dear. I must say, I was tempted to turn up with an armful of ceramics and a tub of adhesive to see if she would actually pack her bags. Oh well, perhaps I had better stick to the washing up.

Mind you, even with washing up, a chore I thought I had forgotten more about than most people will ever know, I was caught out the other day. This came as a surprise to me because the ever critical Mrs H has taught me when to change the water, how to operate with both concentrated and ordinary washing up liquid and on what I may and may not use a scouring pad.

The inroads I can make into a full draining board during a commercial break is awesome and an object lesson to any aspiring dishcloth artist. But there is always something new to learn.

The other evening I had just completed a particularly stimulating session of washing up and, with an arrogant flourish, was rinsing out the dishcloth. At this point, my mentor hove into view. She soon put me in my place and seized the chance to reprogram my memory bank with another piece of information.

"Don't use hot water to do that," she exclaimed as if she had put her hand in something particularly nasty. "The bugs like the warmth. They say 'Hey, come on chaps this is cosy'. You should use cold water." Where would I be without this walking encyclopaedia? There was more to come.

"Did you know," she asked, doing her Michael Caine impression, "There are more germs on a dishcloth than there are in a waste-bin?" I had to admit, that particular gem had passed me by. Just where does she get these snippets from?

I do, in fact, know the answer to that one. These are all facts she has read somewhere and stored up for future reference. If I discover a newspaper folded back or a magazine with the corner of the page turned down, I know there is something new on the way to enhance Fortress life.

Not long ago I spotted a page torn our of the paper which carried the headline, "Broccoli is good for the heart". Sure enough, within days, broccoli was added to the Fortress menu. Mrs H served it up along with a lecture on how it would have our ventricles and aortas functioning well into the next century.

Cereals containing excess sugar are banned. And last week, she produced shreds of decimated newspaper and used the words printed on them to preach to her charges the benefits of extra fruit and fresh vegetables. Somehow, to a twelve and ten year old, their mother's warnings of osteoporosis melt into the background in favour of food of the junk variety.

They are dispatched to school with lunchboxes full of nutrition and fibre plus a flask of unsweetened juice. This, they claim, severely damages their street cred. According to them, all their mates have white bread, crisps and chocolate, not to mention a heavily E numbered carton of drink.

I'm never quite sure if it is eating the food itself that they object to or whether they find it has little or no swap value on the black market.

I did accuse Mrs H of believing everything she reads. "I don't," she insisted. "I take some of it with a pinch of salt." Not in this house dear. Salt increases the risk of heart disease.

She certainly gives little credence to what info I pick up. When she had her bad back a couple of weeks ago, I informed her that I had heard you should not put heat on the sore part but use an ice pack.

"Hmph!" came that endearing equine snort. "I don't care what you've heard. My back wants warmth."

Perhaps Mrs H ought to write a book of helpful hints. Or even produce a video nasty on how a woman should run a successful household. Ah, I can see one problem here. Not every woman will be fortunate enough to have an amiable workhorse like me.

MAINTAIN AT ALL TIMES A FULL KETTLE

Another new rule, "Maintain a full kettle" has now been added to the Fortress statute book. This was given Royal Assent by Mrs H when I had the effrontery to use the kettle to make a cup of coffee just before she wanted it.

I was made aware that I had done something that caused displeasure when the equine snort was delivered as, clutching my beverage, I was making good my escape from the kitchen. Immediately I apologised, then waited to learn what I had done wrong.

"Who's been using the kettle?" demanded Mrs H knowing full well that it was me. I confessed that in my efforts to prepare a hot drink, yes, I had taken the innovative step of using the kettle.

"I'm sorry," she said haughtily, "but I always maintain a full kettle so it's ready for next time." She said this as if I was the only being ever to have been discharged from the womb with a faulty set of natural instincts.

Of course, it's all very well having these rules if everybody sticks to them. Especially the one who dreams them up. It wasn't many hours before I went to use the kettle again and it was empty. You know who hadn't filled it up. When challenged she said, "Well I only do it when I'm cooking."

Since we're on the subject of sticking to the rules I must take this opportunity to deny the propaganda Mrs H is spreading that I am responsible for her acquiring what amounts to a criminal record. She has been fined for overdue library books. I am, of course, to blame. She has even convinced those nice ladies in the local library that I was the cause of her indiscretion. As I was not there to defend myself, I must set the record straight.

Mrs H has four books out of the library. She does not choose ordinary books that the average human being can manage. No, they are big thick cookery books and there were a couple weighty tomes on computers.

Now, because her time is so taken up just keeping pace with life, she rarely has a moment to glance at these books. Consequently, for some months, they have been spending three weeks languishing beside her bed followed by a trip to the library to be renewed.

This is a minor task to one consumed with such day to day

worries as what to wear in the hot weather. So, muggins here usually heaves them to the library when I change the one book that I am allowed to read in my limited downtime.

Last time I had to go to the library was in the middle of Mrs H's three weeks. I informed her that I wouldn't take her books as I would have to lug them around the bookshelves while I choose a new one for myself. I told her they were not due for another week. Here is where our logic differs.

Mrs H was babbling away one evening. I do admit that I was on autopilot for most of it, releasing the odd perfunctory grunt so she could rabbit on in the belief that I was riveted. However, I was tuned in when she was spouting about the library.

"I went to the library today," she said. There then followed one of her fulsome stories on what happened. It was a bit like a Famous Five adventure without the "lashings of ginger beer".

Anyway, as my defence, I put it to you that it is reasonable to assume that if Mrs H had visited the library, she would have taken her books to be renewed.

Apparently not. She only went in to get another book out. So, as she paid her fine she announced that it was my fault for not bringing them back when I took my book in and "I bet he won't put this in the paper."

What makes it worse is that I'm in enough trouble with the libraryites as it is. It seems that every time I go to the library, their computer goes down. Last time I entered the building I was greeted by a throng of people hugging piles of books waiting to be processed.

A couple of harassed library assistants were appealing for calm. As soon as I was spotted one of them pointed an accusing finger at me and announced: "It's his fault." Really! I take the blame for enough things at home without being the fall guy for the library computer.

I'll get even with them. They often skive off to this little room at the back of the counter. I'll find out what they get up to in there and tell their boss. Actually, I bet I know what they do. They're making sure they've got a full kettle.

COULD I FIND WORDS FOR MRS H'S BIRTHDAY? OH YES

Mrs H has just moved another year nearer free prescriptions. Once again I had trouble getting a suitable birthday card. Either I can find a picture I like but the words don't suit or the other way round. If I do hit upon one where the words and picture fit the bill, you can bet your life it's the only one in the rack that hasn't got an envelope with it.

It seems I always choose the same period in my lunch hour as everyone else to go into greetings card shops. And what is more, they 're hovering around the same section I want. There I am at the back, ducking and weaving trying to get a glimpse of a card. Rather like trying to attract the landlords attention in a crowded bar.

Something that gets my goat is the number of women who look at cards intended for men to send to women. I know Mrs H does because she said to me once, "I saw a lovely card you could send to me when it's my birthday."

I did try to find out why she does this. She came out with a typical female answer. "I do not actively do it." No, I don't really know what that means either. It would hardly be a defence in court for your action.

"Yes Your Honour. I did point the shotgun over the counter and demand money. But I didn't actively do it."

As with many other aspects of life at Fortress Haverson, there are strict guide-lines as to the cards I may and may not buy. Large illustrations of flowers that look as though they were painted by Brat Minor during his early period are not particularly well received. Nor are such pictures as two cuddling teddy bears, looking as though they are trying to sustain each other through a severe bout of dysentery.

Cards in pastel colours with elegant ladies are permitted as are cute animals such as kittens. I do not buy the latter as they open that old debate that Fortress Haverson would be a richer place if we had a cat. I'm at the bottom of the pack now when the pile is constructed solely of humans. To come below a feline would really shatter a chap's self respect.

I have to be careful with the words too. Slushy verbiage is not her and it wouldn't sound right coming from me. After twenty two years of marriage, some of the verses just don't seem appropriate.

Here is a selection of verses that I rejected during my card hunting.

"You ask me why I care so much. Its because you are so dear."

Dear? What do they mean by that? Am I supposed to enclose a recent bank statement emphasise the point?

"I never thought I could love you more than I did. But each day I discover new reasons for loving you more."

A new one each day? And does this mean such discoveries as, "Oh my word, Aubergine Bake for tea. That's another reason for loving you more than I did yesterday."

"Every thought I have of you is a happy one."

At 3.29 a.m., in the early hours of Wednesday morning, I was awoken abruptly as Mrs H heaved herself out of bed and stumbled off to the loo. My thoughts were not happy ones.

Perhaps, in future, I should design my own card. It would be shaped like an open hand Marigold. Pictured in the palm of the hand would be an amiable chap projecting loyalty, honesty and trust. Yes indeed, rather like the picture that accompanies this column. Wording across the fingers of the hand would read, "Happy birthday to the woman I try to please."

On opening the card, there will be a border round the edge comprising drawings of domestic objects. A paint roller, a washing up bowl and garden tools spring readily to mind. And what about the wording?

"Your birthday gives me the chance to say
you are my inspiration.
If I fall behind with the jobs I do,
you provide the motivation.
I mow the lawn and paint the walls
and bravely clear the guttering.
With patience I wait when we're going out
And hope you can't hear me muttering
Each day I strive to get it right
My devotion couldn't be plainer
So love to you on your special day
From your faithful old retainer."

There was one card I almost bought. It was white with an oval on the front in which was a picture of a defiant tulip. There was just a short message inside which said simply this. "I can't put into words what I feel about our life together."

Oh yes I can.

A MYSTERIOUS SMELL HALTS MRS H'S IRONING

It has taken these last couple of weeks to get the brain back in gear after a two week break. The holiday itself has become a vague dream I once had. In fact it went into soft focus within about an hour of being back behind my desk.

Even the stresses of the holiday don't seem so bad now as they did at the time. Stresses like the evening we were down to our last few pounds and desperation set in as the hole in the wall kept spitting my card out in disgust. Fortunately it was due only to the absence of a computer link.

Then the vague Brat Minor left his camera in a restaurant and lost his wallet in a busy street. Amazingly both were recovered intact. Sadly he has learnt nothing from the experience. As I write he is combing Fortress H for the keys to the garden shed which he has absentmindedly put down somewhere.

I had trouble getting going from the moment we arrived home. After a long drive, the last thing I felt like doing was heaving suitcases out of the boot. Wearily, we dumped everything in a giant heap in the north wing, extracting only the essentials.

Brats served no useful purpose at this stage of the holiday. Having grudgingly assisted with the unloading their only contribution was to create even greater chaos by plundering suitcases and bags to get at the goodies they had bought.

Of course, Mrs H was soon firing on all cylinders, clearing up the aftermath. After a couple of idle weeks, the washing machine was about to be pressed into almost round the clock activity.

But even Mrs H was having trouble with her organisation. The starting of the washing machine for at least the first three loads was followed almost immediately by her notorious penetrating shriek.

When we were first married, this scream used to have me rushing to her aid in the belief that, at the very least, she had stood on a rusty nail. I have since learnt that it is a combination of frustration and anger. As I am usually the cause of this potent mixture I now keep well out of the way.

These particular shrieks were followed by a drumming of feet as Mrs H pounded in the direction of the kitchen. Her mission to get the washing machine door open before it took on too much water as additional garments kept coming to light that needed the current wash programme.

Mrs H strove to restore Fortress H to its workman-like lifestyle but her luck failed to improve. We ended up stepping on the type of banana skin that only falls in the path of a Haverson.

At the best of times, Mrs H seems to spend every spare moment with the iron clamped in her right hand. With a backlog of holiday washing to beat into submission she was virtually ironing in her sleep.

During her first assault on the pile of crumpled clothes, we smelt an unpleasant aroma. It was not the ironing board or the clothes. She put her nose close to the iron to sniff out the source of the problem. In so doing she came eye to eye with a spider that had set up camp in the water compartment of the steam iron. He was now being gently marinated.

The notable Mrs H shriek has, in the past, summoned me to capture spiders from some unusual parts of Fortress H. None can compare with a spider trapped in the steam iron.

Fortunately, this spider having gone to that great web in the sky, was in no position to trigger Mrs H's phobia. Fortunately, for me that is, I suspect the spider may have had other views.

It may sound easy to eject a spider from such a hiding place. but no matter how we shook and waggled the iron, it refused to yield the body of it's departed eight-legged resident. Bits of wire were pressed into service but 24 hours later the spider was still entombed in the iron.

By now Mrs H was beginning to panic. The airing cupboard was bulging. A measure of her desperation can be gained from the fact that, much against her better judgement, she allowed me to dismantle the appliance. I succeeded in isolating the water chamber but there was no way in.

The smell of boiling spider was so awful and would only get worse so we had no alternative but to make the iron redundant, at least temporarily. At present, the spider is lying in state in its plastic tomb on the kitchen work surface. Visitors to Fortress H are led past it to prove this unlikely tale is true and to pay their respects.

I did not pay my respects. I had to pay for a new iron.

DON'T WAKE ME. I'M HAVING SUCH A NICE DREAM

Shut-down of Fortress Haverson at night comes in about three phases. The first hint of calm descends when the children are finally persuaded to go to bed. But the sand man knows not to visit yet. Mrs H will maintain the pace for a good while longer.

When even she has had enough, there is still this period before we go to bed when we are in limbo. I am ready for a good kip but, having had me at her disposal all night, Mrs H will suddenly decide to discuss the issues of the day.

Sleep is put on hold while I hear about the three piece suite she's seen and get an update on how far behind I am with all the outstanding decorating. Eventually, she runs out of steam and I can dive between the sheets.

Oh, that lovely warm feeling that comes over you in waves when you've had a tiring day and you snuggle under the duvet. Your body unwinds and you almost purr with contentment. I had just gone through this ecstasy barrier the other night and was settling into my book for a few minutes relaxing reading before slipping into unconsciousness. Into a world where I am out of reach even of Mrs H.

I had read no more than a couple of sentences when I was jerked back to reality. The Fortress Dynamo entered the room. I say entered but it was more of an assault.

"I'm not sleeping in this bed with that thing in here. It will keep me awake all night." At first I thought Mrs H was having a conversation with somebody else about me. Then I noticed she was armed with a fly swat. She began leaping around issuing blood-curdling wails and thwacking innocent parts of the room.

The fly ducked and weaved pursued by a determined Mrs H. She executed perfect forehand drives with the fly swat but failed to execute the fly. Every time she paused there would be a brief silence before the buzzing started again.

"Aaarrgh! I can't stand it," screeched Mrs H. She embarked on another swashbuckling circuit of the bedroom, pausing only to give the curtains a particularly savage pounding. My pre-sleep wallow was interrupted beyond recall. Why, I thought to myself as the pantomime continued, do I put up with this woman. Who else would lie patiently in bed while their demented wife behaved like a knight who had trapped his delicate bits in his chain mail?

It was an odd coincidence that I should have such thoughts of putting up with Mrs H at this particular time. I had just spoken to her sister on the phone who had informed me that her husband had this strange dream. He dreamt that I had left Mrs H.

"You got fed up with all the nagging," she explained. My brother-in-law says that details of the dream are fading but he did piece the bare bones of it together.

It seems that Mrs H was sounding off to her sister about me. Of all things, my washing up was one of her gripes. While she was in full flight, apparently I turned on my heel and walked out, stating, "I've had enough of this."

Mrs H's sister could not believe what was happening but her husband assured her. "I could see it coming. He was near the end of his tether." When she heard the tale,

Mrs H was singularly unimpressed.

"I don't call it nagging," she snorted. " I call it reminding." Call it what you like but I wonder whether she is asking herself if dreams really do come true. There are one or two things she could look sharp about and put into practise that might just delay any impending departure I may have in mind.

Let's have a little less of the "If you put your socks out to wash inside out, that's the way you will get them back." And when she gives me a choice of something, perhaps she could actually do what I ask. Like her suggestions for tea the other night.

"Would you like pizza or shall I do something with that fresh broccoli?"

"Pizza please."

"I think I'll use the broccoli." Why bother to ask? And what ever she does for tea, perhaps it could, in future, be available while I'm still hungry and not when my stomach has been denied so long, I have lost my appetite.

Perhaps the message of this dream is that I have been taken for granted for far too long. It's time I was cosseted. I look forward to a few more comments like this.

"No dear. You stay there. I'll see if they locked the shed after they put their bikes away. You've had a hard day, I'll make the coffee. Tell you what. Why don't you pop up the pub while I cut the lawn."

Now who's dreaming.

MRS H FLUMMOXED BY A FRIDGE MAGNET

Mrs H is not easily confused. However, I achieved a notable distinction a few weeks ago when I managed to bring a hint of doubt to her eyes. Her face forms a fascinating picture when she thinks I may have got one over on her. The brow becomes furrowed and the lips pout. She issues a series of truncated grunts as she starts to say something then changes her mind before a complete word can be formed.

I succeeded in confusing her when I spotted a fridge magnet in a gift shop. Motivated by infantile humour I dived in and bought it for her. It sported the following message. "Dull women have immaculate homes".

At first she chuckled then you could almost here the cerebral cogs turning as she tried to decide what message I was sending out. Was I saying Fortress H is a tip but she is a little raver? Or maybe I was suggesting that she is as boring as the house is tidy.

I have to admit that with Mrs H I have probably got the best of both worlds. In general she is well organised and always has been. Her father tells me that when she lived at home he had no sooner put his newspaper down than his eldest daughter would appear from nowhere to tidy it away.

Fortress H is kept in good nick. Especially considering the younger inmates posses a natural ability to undermine their mothers attempts to keep the place presentable.

On the other hand, she is far from dull. Anybody who has been on the receiving end of one of her animated accounts of what would otherwise be an everyday occurrence will know this.

I arrived home from work the other night to be greeted by a welcome that consisted of, "Hello. You'll never guess what some idiot did when I was driving through the village this morning." The plot of the story that followed told how a motorist had driven alongside an orderly queue of traffic and cut up Mrs H to get back in the correct lane.

The tale itself was dramatised for the retelling and embraced pedestrians, the prevailing driving conditions plus every thought that went through Mrs H's brain throughout the incident. Her hands and arms were employed to the full to simulate the manoeuvres of the vehicles and emphasise graphically the sheer horror of the situation. I felt like I was the victim of third party road rage.

I do wonder how she sees me. I don't think I would be awarded the "immaculate home" tag. I stagger up to bed some nights to find a pile of odds and ends on my side of the duvet. She will have served notice on me that there is an unacceptable amount of "your rubbish" lying around and that it will become bin fodder if I don't sort it. The pile on the bed is her way of issuing the final warning.

I know she considers me dull at times. This goes back to our early days when she battled hard to part me from my pint of ale in a cosy pub in favour of a going to a disco. I could find no pleasure in going to a place where the lighting was such that visibility was reduced to a few feet, except when strobes flashed violently, inducing a mass migraine.

Communication was out of the question. The volume of the music was clearly intended to attack the central nervous system. And, most serious of all, the beer was overpriced.

No doubt my offspring also have an opinion of their father. Mind you, it would appear Brat Minor has little to say on the subject. Last week, everyone in his class had to speak for thirty seconds on a subject nominated by the teacher. Knowing his teacher, I have a suspicion it was no coincidence that Brat Minor was given the topic. "Your Father".

Now, I devote money and time in vast quantities to this young man but by his own admission, he struggled to fill thirty seconds with a eulogy to his dad. He told them where I work, that I try to be funny but I'm not, I won't let him and his sister have a cat and that in general I am a "pain in the bottom".

When he reported the details of his maiden speech, I noticed his mother did not contradict him on any point. Anyway, I wouldn't turn to her for support because I know she can fill considerably more than thirty seconds on the subject of her husband. I've listened to her expanding on the topic before. Many times.

Perhaps she ought to get me a fridge magnet which reads, "Dull husbands make good listeners".

TECHNOLOGY HAS ITS HAZARDS

We have gone cordless. I have made a rash investment in a cordless telephone, simply to get peace and quiet when taking or making a call. Now, when you telephone Fortress Haverson, you can let your imagination run riot wondering which room we are in.

With the wretched thing fixed in the hall, the chances of making an uninterrupted call were zero. Brats are incapable of doing anything without generating noise. Even a harmless game of snakes and ladders can degenerate into a brawl with accusations of dice fiddling and snake abuse.

It seems necessary to shout at a Brat approximately every 2 minutes or discipline breaks down completely. It is not helpful to have this din going on in the background – particularly if it's a call where you need to concentrate, like trying to deal with an insurance company to extract the most favourable motor premium.

"No accidents in the last 5 years and... WILL YOU KEEP THE NOISE DOWN... sorry about that. What did you say? Oh, my wife's date of birth. Let me see now, she was born in 19... I SHAN'T TELL YOU AGAIN..." and so it goes on.

Now I can take the phone into a vacant room and hear myself think. I can even go into the garage and make a call or clamber up into the spider-infested loft where no one dare venture to disturb me.

I should point out that there are some disadvantages in this liberation. To the younger inmates, the phone has become an attractive means of chatting with their friends without shifting their idle carcasses. More than once I have gone to use the phone and found it missing.

On one occasion I found Brat Minor languishing in the bath with it. But usually it is Brat Major, stretched out on her bed, discussing the latest high school hunk with a mate.

"Just checking what homework we had to do," she says, hastily putting her hand over the mouth piece.

"I thought you had history. I don't remember a King of England called Wayne."

Incoming calls too can pose a problem. Most of the calls are indeed for Brat Major so she is usually first to the phone. But if the call is for me or Mrs H, the dear child carts the phone to where ever we are and bangs it down in front of us with a dismissive, "For you". We could be having a meal, painting the wall or performing Scottish Country Dancing for all she cares.

There follows a tense exchange twixt parent and daughter. Parent tries to establish who is on the line without letting the caller know they are there. Daughter seizes the opportunity to embarrass parent by replying at full volume.

"Who is it?" The question is hissed through clenched teeth.

"Didn't catch the name."

"Who did they ask for?" Parent is now red in the face with the effort to continue eating the meal while injecting anger into the question but without increasing decibels

"Dunno." With that she turns on her heel and leaves the chosen parent to swallow a mouthful of piping hot Aubergine Bake, pick up the phone and make some effort to have a coherent conversation.

One other drawback to phones of the cordless variety is that, to obtain best reception, a telescopic aerial has to be extended. This can be a lethal weapon. If a Brat zooms past in search of a secluded place to take a call and, someone is foolish enough to be in the way, they are likely to have an eye whipped out.

I have mentioned before Mrs H's professed hatred of the phone. This continues to puzzle me. How can she loath it so much yet spend all that time using it. In fact I think she sees me rather like the telephone. She moans about me most of the time but makes sure she gets her money's worth.

Anyway, the arrival of the cordless communicator has taken her into new spheres. She still curses when the phone rings but now the constant pull towards the common good can be sustained without interruption.

Using that talent exclusive to women which enables them to concentrate on at least two things at once, she continues to perform the task in hand while holding a conversation. The other night, she was on the phone to her father and cleaning the oven at the same time.

The fact that she is now able to take phone calls "on the hoof", means, unfortunately, she can maintain her monitoring of what we other inmates are up to. Previously, Mrs H on the phone meant down tools, plunder the biscuit tin and flick the telly over to the raunchy film on Channel 4.

Now, with the phone clamped to her ear, she patrols the house like someone from Group 4. The only difference is, Mrs H doesn't let anyone escape.

I WAS NOT THE PLANK IN QUESTION

The Fortress bank account is unwell. It sustained a severe bruising in the great back-to-school spend last month. It was particularly crippled because Brat Major moved to the High School. A new uniform, PE kit, football boots and goodness knows what else have left me scratching around to find finance for the bare essentials such as the price of a pint.

Having invested in all this gear, Mrs H was brought to boiling point only a couple of days into the term when a sheepish student submitted the new school trousers to the Fortress sewing department with a hole in the knee.

"I fell over," protested the cowering Brat Major as her mother raged at her daughter's lack of care and gave a passionate speech on the price of school uniforms.

Among the many purchases Mrs H made for the new term were trainers. Now, trainers come in pairs and it is normal for those pairs to be a left foot and a right foot that match in design and colour. All right, I know that's not rocket science but remember, it's Mrs H we're dealing with here.

In fairness, to her, she got some of it right. They were a pair consisting of a left foot and a right foot. Indeed they were more or less the same colour. But each shoe was of a quite different design. It gets worse.

Mrs H's jaw moves with ease when she goes into talk mode but even I have never seen it lower so swiftly than when she was informed that she had bought odd trainers. Shocked into honesty she went on to admit that she had taken them out of the box, cleaned them with a protective spray and marked her daughter's name on the tongue of each and still not noticed.

Actually, Brat Major was just as bad really. She plodded around the house in them to soften them up but didn't spot the difference until she got them to school and was changed ready for gym.

Mrs H has, of course, made it clear that she was not at fault. It was the poor lad who served her. Maybe so, but who can blame him. The shop was busy and he was trying to deal with other harassed mothers and their truculent offspring at the same time as assisting the formidable duo of Mrs H and Brat Major. They can't agree on the weather let alone a pair of trainers.

Mrs H rang the shop. She received an apology and they offered to put the matter right. But guess who was charged with the task of taking them back?

I didn't want them to think I was the plank who bought them so I carefully rehearsed my speech. I sought out an assistant a good distance from any other signs of civilisation and explained the problem.

"My wife bought these on Saturday." I stressed. Fortunately I was served by a sympathetic lady. Mind you, I am not sure whether her sympathies were directed at the inconvenience we had suffered or at me for the person I had married.

I do have to say that Mrs H is not too enamoured with one of my recent sorties into the shopping game. Our faithful old alarm clock has no battery back-up in case of a power cut. So, when Brat Minor's radio alarm gave up the ghost, we decided to give him ours and buy a new one.

The clock we bequeathed to our son is a friendly old thing. It has a considerate bleeper that brought us gently to consciousness. Dreams faded away rather than came to an abrupt end. The new one, although of the same make and design has a twisted sadistic streak.

It has a bold display that almost leers at me when I get into bed as if to say, "Ha. It won't be long before I have you out of there again." I can imagine its microchips crackling with anticipation all night at the prospect of sounding reveille.

When the waking hour arrives it howls with ecstasy. I am stung into action to get it switched off before a window shatters. Its penetrating bleeper is such that I feel I ought to be leading the family out to the Anderson Shelter.

Mrs H is unimpressed. She is not at her best around dawn. With the old alarm she used to come to in her own good time. Now, by the time I have silenced the squawking machine, the human being adjacent to me has her head buried in the pillow muttering oaths I didn't think she knew.

She hasn't suggested it yet but if she decides the alarm has to be changed, I'm not taking it back. There is no way I will walk into a shop and say, "I'd like to change this alarm please. It keeps waking my wife up in the morning."

NO HIDING PLACE FROM HI-TECH MRS H

I sometimes wonder what Mrs H gets up to in the car. For example, the effort she puts into her footwork when she changes gear must be phenomenal. She keeps presenting me with the rubber off the clutch pedal. It's a bit like a boomerang. Every time I put it on again, she brings it back.

And the buckle on the seat-belt gets twisted round the wrong way. It takes ages to work it back. I just don't know how she does it.

Probably the biggest mystery is the interior light. I looked out of the window one night, after Mrs H had parked and locked the car and, to my surprise, the interior light was flashing on and off. It was like a beacon, as if the car had developed its own early warning system to alert other motorists that Mrs H was on the loose. We never have found out what caused it.

Of course, Mrs H thinks everything is perfectly normal. I overheard her on the phone during the week discussing someone who is well past their three score years and ten but is still as sharp as a razor. Mrs H was offering her thoughts on when she gets near her sell by date.

"I don't mind getting old as long as my brain is still functioning," she mused. Then she became aware of my sniggering presence. "He's laughing at me," she announced indignantly down the phone. Well, I couldn't help it. Perhaps I should have reminded her of her mental state one Sunday recently.

It began a normal Sunday, lived according to Fortress law. Six days shalt thou labour. On the seventh thou shalt do a sight more. I had been inflicting the vegetable patch with its autumn dig when I was summoned to the Fortress kitchen. Awaiting me was the usual "could you just do" list so I wouldn't miss out on making my contribution to Sunday lunch.

This involved helping with the vegetables, laying the table, keeping the washing up going and galvanising reluctant Brats into activity. I was even directed to peel the potatoes. I am not usually allowed to wield a potato peeler in anger. By the time I have finished I can turn a good sized potato into little more than a marble.

Once the meal was over, I did a bit of washing up but then I made my excuses and slunk off to the garden to finish my digging. I had been grafting for about half an hour when Mrs H suddenly appeared and demonstrated just what a firm grip she has on her faculties.

"I've finished clearing up," she announced and giving me a perfunctory nod, turned on her heel and headed back to the house. Was she trying to make a point here?

"'Scuse me," I called to her disappearing back, "Did you make this rare appearance in the vegetable patch just to tell me that?".

"Oh. Err... no," she said. There was a pause and her brow furrowed as she fought to regain control of her brain. "I came to see if you wanted a cup of coffee." This really was most unusual. Two rarities in one day. First she had found the way all by herself to this remote part of the garden. Now, not only was I allowed a break but positively encouraged to take it with an offer way out of character. I accepted.

"All right then," she replied . "You can come in and make it." What? Had she come out just to tell me I could have a cup of coffee if I made it? My puzzled look was enough to prompt her to engage brain once again.

"Oh, no. I didn't mean it like that. I meant I'm making one. I'll put the coffee in the cup and boil the kettle. Then, if you're busy now, you can come in and make it when you're ready." At last. Brain and mouth were finally operating in harmony.

She hasn't yet twigged that our cordless phone could have saved her that trip into the garden. It has an intercom facility. As long as I have the handset with me she can press a button on the base which will alert me with a soothing warble to the fact that she requires my services. I press a button at my end to be connected live to Mrs H. Now she can reprogram me without leaving the house.

That is, of course, if I am within 100 metres of Fortress Haverson. I am beginning to worry that she will take more drastic steps if I stray out of range. Perhaps she'll try to monitor my whereabouts by having me electronically tagged.

I suppose, if she gets really carried away, even the garden may no longer be a place of sanctuary. I can just see her now, pin-pointing my hiding place in the shed with her thermal imaging equipment.

COULD THERE BE A SECOND MRS H OUT THERE

Mrs H looked me hard in the eye and fired a question. In a flash I had this vision of a prosecuting solicitor. You've seen them on TV. They lead the witness down a carefully planned route. Then, to create a bit of drama, they take a couple of paces towards the jury before swinging round and triumphantly delivering the clinching question.

In my case, Mrs H skipped the formality of a cross examination. As I entered the room she had her back to me sorting through some dirty washing. She wheeled round when she heard me and in her best "j'accuse" voice cried, "Why have you been wearing your best after-shave for work?" As she awaited my answer she waved exhibit A. This consisted of one striped shirt, blue, recently worn and giving off a pleasant aroma.

"I could smell it as soon as I lifted the lid of the dirty linen basket," she persisted. I just stood and stared. Were doubts entering her mind suggesting I had another woman? I allowed the pause to become slightly more pregnant before answering.

"That," I replied scornfully, "is the body spray you choose for me and which I have been wearing on and off for weeks."

"Well you must be overdoing it then. It's really powerful." With that the matter was closed. You will note there was no suggestion of an admission that she might have been wrong.

Nevertheless, it did a chap's ego a bit of good to know that she may even have thought another woman would look at me so when the opportunity arose to cast further doubts in her mind, I thought I'd have a bit of sport.

I discovered a lipstick in the back of the car. I carried it into the house as if it was the head of a stampeding buffalo I had shot while on safari.

"Found this in the back of the car," I announced smugly. I stepped back and waited for the interrogation.

"Oh it probably belongs to your daughter," she said dismissively and went about her business.

"I thought you might think I'd had another woman in the car," I said with a hint of disappointment. I was rewarded with her equine snort.

"Umph! If you had had another woman in the car you wouldn't have brought that in. You would have thrown it away and not said anything." Curses, foiled again. But at least she must have considered it to have such a reasoned response ready and waiting.

As for me having another woman, well frankly, one's enough. I certainly couldn't handle two. Especially if they were both like Mrs H. Imagine having two of them bombarding you with experiences like the recent tale of the supermarket loo. This was Mrs H at her endearing best.

Here is the saga in her own words. If you want to experience the authentic atmosphere of Mrs H recounting one of her adventures, follow these simple instructions. Read the next few paragraphs at approximately twice the normal speed and in a voice bursting with excitement. Throw in a few explosive cackles of laughter here and there and use the hands and arms as liberally as you can to make the story more graphic. And what ever you do, don't pause for breath. Are you ready? Go!

"I was in the supermarket today, absolutely desperate to go to the loo. Well, you have to go through two doors to get there. I went through the first door and was just going into the toilet when I realised the light was out. Guess what? Couldn't find a switch. Well there was one but it said 'Emergency Test Only'. I wasn't going to turn that one on. Goodness knows what I might have started.

"There was no window so it was absolutely pitch black. Luckily I had that pen torch you bought me for the car in my bag. You know the one so I can see to unlock the car door – are you listening to me? Anyway. would the damn thing work? The only way I could get any light was to keep shaking it. I had to have some light to know where the toilet paper was.

"I managed to go to the loo all right but then I went to wash my hands. Well, I couldn't put the torch down or it would go out and I didn't want to scrabble around the floor of a public loo looking for it – I wish you'd look at me when I'm talking so I know you're listening. Anyway I put it my mouth. That wasn't too clever really since I'd just been holding it on the loo. Then I wanted to comb my hair and put some lipstick on. I could comb my hair all right but how do you put lipstick on with a torch in your mouth?"

No, on second thoughts, there can't possibly be another woman like that.

PICTURE OF DOMESTIC BLISS IN THE SWEET FACTORY

If you had glanced through the kitchen window at Fortress H last week you would have been rewarded with a picture of domestic bliss. A scene which epitomised happy families.

Mother and daughter were doing some cooking. Mischievous young son was nipping in on the blind side, sticking his finger in the mixing bowl and diving for cover. Dad was pottering amiably about doing what he could to help. Turn up the sound and the reality would have been quite different.

Brat Major had announced some weeks earlier that she and a chum were going to have a stall at the Middle School's Christmas Craft Fair. They felt they could make a killing by selling confectionery. Yes, they would be making all the produce themselves but please could they have an injection of parental cash to finance the venture. This would of course be immediately repaid from the enormous profit they were projecting as a result of their ambitious business plan.

And so it came to pass that Brat Major, under the watchful eye of her mother, spent a couple of evenings slaving over a hot stove. Now, too many cooks spoil the broth. When the cooks concerned are Mrs H and Brat Major the broth just doesn't stand a chance. Brat Major made it clear from the start that she did not want her mother assisting. Initially, Mrs H left her to it. But it wasn't long before the little cherub ran into trouble.

"Mum! Is this mixture thick enough?"

"How do you expect me to tell from the bedroom?" Things went downhill rapidly after that.

"Oh woman. Come and tell me if this is cooked."

"I shan't come and help you if you talk to me like that!"

I made the mistake of walking into the midst of all this chaos in the belief that my tea was being prepared. Immediately I was deemed additional labour and seconded to the washing up.

As Brat Major had drawn up the menu, chocolate was a main ingredient in most of the products. I don't know what she put in her mixture but the remains of it clung to the saucepan like fresh tar. I was into serious Brillo in my efforts to remove the sickly goo.

Madam almost ruined her cookies. She took them carefully out of the oven and left them on top of the cooker. A smell of burning alerted her to the fact that she had left a ring on. This, and most other things that went wrong, was of course the fault of "that woman". Even though Mrs H wasn't in the room at the time.

While all this was going on, I was slushing around in washing up water that had assumed the appearance of liquid mud, Foolishly, I raised the issue of my tea. As Mrs H seemed to be on permanent attachment to Brat Major, I found myself not only washing up but also cooking a couple of pizzas.

Finally the goodies were complete. Brat Major's ginger biscuits were, by all accounts, better than her mother's. I can believe this since Mrs H issues hers with a health warning. "Eating these ginger biscuits can seriously damage your teeth."

The day went well and the girls almost sold out. Inevitably, some of the stock was consumed by the manufacturers. I didn't buy anything. It struck me I would be paying twice. Having been conned into parting with money to buy the ingredients in the first place, I refused to shell out again to buy it back in the form of a chocolate drop.

I did patronise the PTA's refreshments and bought Mrs H and me a cup of coffee. Even that wasn't as simple as you might think. Mrs H was ahead of me in the queue. She ordered herself a cup of coffee but for some strange reason, ignored me. When I raised the matter, she became quite indignant.

"How was I to know you didn't want tea or something?" she demanded. Now I cannot remember the last time I went for a snack with Mrs H and had anything other than coffee. Of course, I was on a looser. Typically, the serving wenches behind the counter were all on her side.

"That's right ," they cooed in support of Mrs H. "You're not a mind reader are you?" There was one lone voice which came to my defence. It was that of Posh End, the former neighbour who moved to the "upmarket part of the village". But being another mere male, nobody took any notice of him. I would add that Mrs H had no difficulty in being in harmony with her husband when it came to who was going to pay.

By the way, if you bought anything from Brat Major's stall, try not to think about who made them as you enjoy your feast. Let me just say this. I know where the fingers that made those truffles have been.

SOCCER AFTERNOON GETS THE BOOT

Not since there was a tax imposed on them in the seventeenth century can windows have caused more grief than they did at Fortress Haverson last Sunday. They prevented me seeing the first goal in the Norwich/Ipswich derby match.

Knowing the game was live on television, I decided the best way to get to see it was to earn time off for good behaviour. I started immediately after breakfast. I washed up and strode into the cold morning air where I defied hypothermia and plunged my hands into a bucket of freezing cold water and washed the car.

I swept up leaves and tidied the shed. But I realised I was out of sight and out of mind. My industry would not be registering with she who matters. So I decided to catch up on one or two jobs that had been hanging around for a while. Surely that would ingratiate me with Mrs H. Some bits and pieces that we had all been stumbling over because I had failed to put them in the loft were swiftly dispatched above ceiling level.

Next I took a light lunch. Then, pausing only to wash up once again I attacked a faulty catch that had been making it difficult to close a window. I dismantled it and reassembled it. Admittedly my labours had no effect whatsoever on making it easier to close the window but at least I had done something.

It was now 2.20 p.m. Kick off at 3 p.m. Mrs H spotted me removing my working togs.

"So you're not going to clean the windows then? I've been asking you for weeks to do them. They're filthy. What ever must people think?"

On went my old anorak again. Out came the bucket to be filled with more freezing water and at 2.25 p.m. I ventured forth into the abrasive afternoon air. I slaved like fury, slopping water indiscriminately at the house in my efforts to complete the task as quickly as possible. By 2.50 p.m. I had done the ground floor. Just enough time to dry off, change, put the kettle on and settle down for the match.

"That was quick!" was the greeting I received from the foreman.

"I haven't done the upstairs ones. I'll do them next weekend." Wrong!

"It was the upstairs ones I most wanted you to do. I can do the downstairs ones. Besides, what's the point in doing the bottom ones first. When you do the upstairs ones all the water will drip down on the ones you've just cleaned."

"All right, all right. I'll go and do them," I said testily, looking pointedly at my watch.

"No, no. You don't have to. But I have been asking you for weeks."

"I'll do them," I insisted irritably. "I can tell you're not very pleased." I headed for the door yet again. Mrs H replied with one of her gems.

"You don't have to do them," she shouted after me with some hostility. "You're not my employee. You're my husband." That's very true. By law employees should get notice of alterations to their terms and conditions. Husbands get no advanced warning at all. In fact they are expected to anticipate sudden changes.

I was beginning to hate that bucket. I filled it with water and got out my old ladder. It is one section of a wooden extending ladder. Such is it's age that it is impossible to ascend and descend without ones hands becoming riddled with splinters.

I must have looked as though I was on fast forward as I shinned up the ladder polished furiously before slithering to the ground, howling with pain at the lacerations to my hands and hastening to the next window.

At 3.10 p.m. I finished. As I approached the back door Brat Major stuck her head out to inform me that Norwich had just scored. I entered Fortress H with a face as black as thunder.

"Your father's not very pleased with me," I heard Mrs H comment to a passing Brat. I settled down to watch the game. By half time I had mellowed and when Mrs H said, "Oh if it's half time could you just get my washing in?" I went without fuss.

My mood changed when I arrived back to be told, "Dad, you've just missed the replay of the Norwich goal." Chuntering to myself that I would have to wait until the post match analysis to see it, I sunk into the sofa for the second half.

After the game had finished, the panel of experts were giving their views as the highlights were replayed. Any minute now I would see the goal. Suddenly the door opened and Mrs H breezed in brandishing a duster.

"Ah, good. The football's finished," she said with satisfaction. "I'll watch the Clothes Show while I clean in here." With that she flipped the TV onto BBC1.

Sometimes I wish I was an employee and not a husband.

STEREOPHONIC NAGGING IS JUST TOO MUCH

We were sitting at the dinner table. I was immersed in my own thoughts. Suddenly, my brain was inserted into gear by a familiar rebuke.

"Are you listening to me?" Obediently I focused on Mrs H, wide eyed and alert as if I had been hanging on her every word. But, to my surprise, she was taking no notice of me whatsoever. I was horrified to discover that it was my daughter who had barked out the reprimand.

This is too much. I know children learn by imitation but I don't think I can handle stereophonic nagging. A few days later there was another incident. We were just leaving Fortress H in the car. Mrs H was going through all the usual pre-flight checks.

"Was the cooker off? Did you shut the toilet window? You're sure everything was switched off?" She received the usual reply which, in two words, expressed all the monotony of the situation.

"Yes dear." The only difference was, it wasn't me that said it. It was Brat Minor. When he was chastised by his mother for being cheeky, he protested furiously.

"But that's what Dad always says." His mother pointed out that she was well aware of that fact and he got on her chimes saying it with such patient suffering so she could live without her son doing it as well. He would serve an appropriate penance if he did it again.

The problem here is that it becomes increasingly difficult to find suitable punishments when they cross the frontiers of acceptable behaviour. Gone are the days when confiscating a favourite toy or putting chocolate and sweets on the forbidden list have much effect.

Homework has become the latest activity that demands a need for a variety of incentives. Given a week to do something they would leave it until the last minute if parental pressure didn't eventually wear them down. Favourite TV programmes are banned and youth club is put on hold until jolly things like spelling and why volcanoes erupt have been set down in best handwriting.

We do get involved with them in doing their homework. Do they appreciate it? Oh no. All they do is argue with us and tell us we're old. Brat Minor had to find a short poem to recite in front of the class. Everything Mrs H came up with was "boring and naf."

And Mrs H herself rejected my suggestion of the catchy piece of metre describing the attributes of a young man from Porthcawl, as inappropriate. Finally he settled on a poem which extolled the virtues of school holidays and condemned the rigours of term time.

On to the next crisis. He had to go to school dressed as a character from a book. Again all our suggestions fell on stony ground. Eventually he plumped for a book about a boy who was mad on computers. This didn't tax the Fortress costume department much but the Blue Peter section burned the midnight oil in an attempt to produce a laptop computer from a bit of cardboard and some sticky tape.

Brat Major, being that bit older, stretches the brain much more with her homework. Some of it frightens me. She appears on occasions to be doing subjects I did just before I left school. I must say I find it all rather interesting but of little use. I don't think there are too many people who would want to listen to me speaking at length on Kinetic Energy or explaining what Order of Symmetry is.

Currently Brat Major's English project is to write a diary based on a trip in a space ship. I was invited to read it. The introduction told how she and another girl made ready for their journey.

"You were allowed to take your parents with you," she wrote. Oh good, I thought. I wonder if she will write me some decent lines. How about, "Dad saved us by grabbing the radio and shouting 'Beam us up Scottie'." But then I read on.

"I couldn't take my parents. They had been killed in a car accident a year ago." What! I demanded an explanation.

"Oh, it would have been just too much hassle to have you along. Telling me what to do all the time."

Of the two, Brat Minor is the most difficult to galvanise into action. Mrs H usually tries counselling him with logic.

"You've only got your Maths and that bit of English to do. If you get on with it now you'll have the rest of the evening to do what you want." She never says that to me.

"You've only got to wash up, clean the windows, put those things in the loft, prune the apple tree, decorate the front room, wash the car, rod the drains and dig the vegetable patch and you've got the rest of 1995 to do what you like."

Not quite the same is it?

SHOPPING HELL AS THE 'H CLAN' CATCH THE GRUMPS

It's a good job I am not Bob Cratchett's employer. With only a couple of days to go I am in a right bah humbug mood about Christmas. The way I feel at the moment, the Ebenezer Scrooge philosophy on Yuletide is eminently appealing.

Shopping is at the root of my grumpy outlook. It started when Mrs H was laid low with the flu. She informed me through a series of snuffles and hacks that I would have to crack on with the present gathering or we'd never be ready for Christmas. She armed me with a festive list and I set about the job of separating myself from vast quantities of money. Then the frustration set in.

Most of the items on my list were either out of stock, the wrong size, or only available on CD ROM – whatever that means. I reported back to base on my abortive expedition. Mrs H soon came up with the answer. Oh joy. The very next Sunday we were all to go on a family shopping trip.

It turned out to be a bad weekend all round. On the Saturday I travelled some forty miles to play hockey on a cold, foggy afternoon. We got annihilated 6 – 1 and I pulled a hamstring. By Sunday morning my leg had stiffened nicely and hobbling round Norwich was not high on my wish list.

My mood darkened yet further before we left. We had an ugly confrontation with the truculent Brat Major. For reasons best known to herself, she refused to wear a coat. When threatened by her mother she flounced off to the car muttering that she didn't care if she got cold and wet.

It was unfortunate that I was adjacent to Mrs H as she responded to her daughter's petulance. The sensation I experienced in my right ear as I took the full blast of a Mrs H bellow, must be what it is like to be half way up a church steeple when the bell ringers start heaving on the ropes.

Mrs H had her shopping list but, of course, once let loose she seized the opportunity to look at anything and everything. This inflicted maximum boredom on the young Haversons who began arguing and fighting. I just looked on helplessly as my bit of plastic was swiped through that many terminals the magnetic strip must be suffering from metal fatigue.

To add to my woe, practically every shop seemed to have the same tape of Christmas music playing. I lost count of the number of times I heard Bing fantasising about heavy snow on or about the 25th.

To appease the Brats we headed for a well known fast food chain. It seemed everybody else had the same idea. There was nowhere to sit – and my hamstring hurt. Growing more irritable by the second I stumbled around clutching a tray of food for fully ten minutes before we found a table.

Then, when we were halfway through our meal, other desperate diners started to hover, nudging each other and nodding in our direction to indicate that we looked as though we might be leaving soon. I felt quite guilty for having the nerve to finish my coffee.

We returned home fully laden but with few of the items off our original list. And my hamstring hurt.

Time was running out for me to get something for Mrs H so the following Saturday I decided to make a solo raid on the city. Unfortunately, Brat Major muscled in on the act.

It was almost as bad as having her mother with me. I was dragged into clothes shops and made to offer completely ill-informed opinions on what suited a young lady approaching her teens. Was I glad to get home! And my hamstring hurt.

It had only partially recovered by the Saturday evening when it was to be put to the test at the PTA's annual Christmas thrash. Fortunately my dancing is so bad that it was impossible to tell whether I was performing normally or gyrating while hampered through injury. In fact, the odd twinge of the hamstring caused the unintentional injection of a few innovative steps into my normally shambolic dance routine.

The whole family has been a bit grumpy lately. Brat Minor had a hair cut for which he carefully specified the style. He got precisely what he asked for and has whinged constantly ever since because everyone tells him he looks like a monk.

Mrs H got stroppy when she was decorating the tree. Despite her best efforts, all the red lights kept winding up on the same side.

I don't know. Maybe Mrs H will declare an amnesty on major projects over the festive season and I will be put on light duties. It's a dog's life. Perhaps that's something I should point out to her. A husband is for life. Not just for Christmas.

THE JOY OF BEING LEFT HOME ALONE

She can do it. I know because I was there. I have seen Mrs H ready to go out more or less on time. The only trouble was, I didn't get the benefit because I wasn't going with her.

Mrs H's sister had bravely suggested that she and her husband would take our two hooligans to the pantomime. Unfortunately, on the day, she was smitten by a bug so Mrs H was invited to deputise.

I arrived home from work to be greeted by a family busy getting tea and preparing for the off. "We must be ready by half past six." Mrs H blasted out the order as she urged her offspring ever onward. I should add that they were getting their own tea, not mine. I had to do that later.

When Brother-in-law rang the doorbell it was precisely 6.30 p.m. Mrs H and the Brats were just donning shoes and coats. They were ready to leave at 6.34 p.m.

"How come," I demanded as they went out of the door, "You can be ready when somebody else is taking you out but you can never manage it for me?"

"Hmph." The equine snort heralded a strong rebuttal. "We started getting ready in good time," she protested. " It didn't matter who was taking us, we'd have been on time." Ah but would the urgency have been there if the malleable old ox had been the chauffeur?

With that they departed. I bade them farewell with the comment that it goes way beyond the call of duty of a brother-in-law to be seen in public with my family and did he want to dash off a quick placard stating, "These people are nothing to do with me."

I should point out that I could have gone instead of him but the lure of being left home alone was overwhelming and I was quite happy to stand down. My family found this strange. In fact I have to admit that my family seem to find me more than a little odd most of the time. For example, recently Brat Major confided in me that, only the previous day, her brother had been giving a swift assessment of his father. She faithfully reported his words.

"You know," he is alleged to have said. "I think Dad is a different religion to us. He goes mad if we swear but then he'll go and swear himself." I don't know why religion should have a bearing on that. Maybe his Cadfael haircut has changed more than his appearance.

I must set the record straight here. In spite of the fact that they drive me to distraction, I am most careful what words I use when remonstrating with the younger inmates. Even when they have reduced me to a quivering wreck with bulging eyes, purple face and a voice that sounds like an old Ford Cortina that won't start, I have a built in security mechanism in the brain which trips the bad language mouth-link.

I wonder why they are always suggesting I am weird. They complain about my singing, groan at my jokes and poke fun – and fingers – at my waist line. Oddly enough, when it comes to their mother they have a peculiar sort of respect. I think it's driven by fear.

This was well illustrated recently when I put some plates down on top of the microwave. Cadfael observed my actions and commented, "If you'd done that and mum was here you'd be history. We're not allowed to stand anything on the microwave."

I have never heard either of them repeat anything that I have said with such reverence. I wonder if that's because Mrs H talks so much more than I do that sooner or later, some of it is bound to stick in their colander minds.

Oh yes, she does talk a lot and I can support that claim with a statement from a new convert to my way of thinking. None other than her boss. He knew her before he employed her and he told me a couple of weeks ago, "I used to read your column and think, 'That's a side of Mrs H I don't know'. But now I have been working with her for over a year I've come over to your side." He paused before adding, "It wasn't half quiet when she was off with the flu."

He should have been at home. I've still not managed to work out how she managed to cough so much and still fit in her quota of yakking.

I did get one crumb of comfort thanks to two lovely ladies I bumped into in the city recently. They instructed me to tell Mrs H that I am better looking than my picture which accompanies this column. As soon as I got home I informed Mrs H of this boost to my ego.

She laughed. And laughed and laughed.

GAME OF DIY SNAKES AND LADDERS

Brat Major has two great loves in life. One is eating, the other spending money. She incinerates food at meal-time and in between takes on board additional supplies by carrying out raids on the Fortress larder.

She continues to grow and soon she will dwarf her parents. Only last week I couldn't find a pair of my jeans. She had hung them in her wardrobe thinking they were hers.

Money is not so easy as food for her to come by. I suspect her best source is when she has a school dinner. I haven't had any dinner money change for years. In fact this probably satisfies both her cravings. The change is no doubt invested in the school vending machines.

In desperation for some cash the other day she sidled up to me and asked, "Dad. have you any jobs you want doing? Not outside ones. It's too cold to go out there and do anything." This was not an offer born out of her charitable nature. Reward is always discussed before she will get her hands dirty. Anyway, before I could answer, her mother intervened.

"Hmph." Yes the equine snort heralded an opinion from Mrs H. "What jobs can your father give you to do indoors. He doesn't have any inside jobs."

"'Scuse me," I protested. "Who does most of the washing up? Who changed the sheets this week? Who did the vacuuming last..."

"They're my jobs. You just help me with them." Now this is interesting. Do we have Mrs H's views on marriage here? That partnership of give and take?

I do believe we have confirmation of the one way system. Clearly there is a split of responsibilities. Anything within the walls of Fortress Haverson is down to Mrs H with me a resource to be drawn upon as required. Anything beyond the backdoor is my pigeon. However, this is the equivalent of the blue collar area. Mrs H is available to advise but hands on involvement is out of the question. We had a good example of this the other day.

Father Christmas can always be relied upon to deliver something that requires a parent to have a degree in engineering, a working knowledge of electrics and more tools than Do It All. As a rule this means that anything my children get has to wait until a relative can oblige.

This year, Cadfael became the owner of a basketball net and backboard. These had to be screwed to the wall. A straight forward job you might think. Not for me. I put it off for as long as I could, blaming the snow and anything else I could think of. But driven on by Mrs H I finally had to give it a go. She appeared from time to time to supervise.

"Either put it in the middle of the wall or centre it over the window," she instructed. It will look funny from down the garden otherwise."

Oh yes, I can see Brat Minor now. Bouncing the ball towards the net then stopping dead in mid-dribble, his face askance at the lop-sided positioning of the backboard. Why, he'd be too ashamed to invite a friend round. Who'd want to shoot a few baskets with a boy who had a backboard that was off-centre?

I drilled four holes in the board for the screws. OK so far. With a series of lightening calculations, a length of wood, a tape measure and an awl, I measured and marked the position of the board above the window.

I then proceeded to perform an act worthy of the big top. I threaded an extension cable out of a window and plugged in my drill. I scaled my cumbersome metal step ladder which swayed like a soldier on parade about to faint. As I climbed, the cable lovingly wrapped itself round my legs so by the time I reached sufficient height to drill I had got well and truly knotted.

There I was balancing like an acrobat at the top of the step ladder. Trussed up in electrical cable as if about to execute an Houdini-style escape. Amazingly I managed to drill my four holes. Even more astonishing, three of them were in the right place.

In her capacity as foreman Mrs H appeared periodically to offer encouragement. "I don't want that falling on anybody's head," she rasped with a thinly disguised lack of faith in my workmanship. And a little later, "The ball will keep going over the neighbours fence you know. We won't be very popular."

I was almost overcome with the urge to present her with my tools and tell her to get on with it. One of these days I'll muscle in on her domain and oversee the production of the evening meal. On second thoughts, perhaps it's better not to gain too much knowledge of such matters. I can hear her now. "Could you just do us an Aubergine Bake for tea?"

WHAT'S IN A NAME? IT DEPENDS ON WHAT MRS H WANTS

You can't trust 'em can you? You think they do what you tell them but they don't. They say they've cleaned their teeth but just after they've gone to bed, you find a bone dry toothbrush.

Brat Minor will be dispatched to his squat to tidy it up. He could be gone for anything up to an hour. Suddenly we'll become aware that he has returned to the ground floor.

"Have you done your room?" he'll be asked. His reply is usually loaded with indignation. How could anyone contemplate that he hadn't obeyed his mother's orders? A visit to his retreat will reveal a different story. They'll be books and empty cassette cases all over the floor. Subbuteo men that have gone AWOL from the rest of the team and a random selection of clothes, most of which are yearning to get acquainted with the washing machine.

His sister is no better. The main difference with her room is that every nook and cranny will be playing host to a hastily hidden chocolate wrapper. The other night I went into her bedroom when she was supposed to be asleep. Surely no one could sleep comfortably while contorted like that.

I moved closer. Was that the merest hint of a smile on her lips? I slid my hand under the pillow. The smile became a grin and yes, my forage was rewarded with a fist full of half munched crisps.

You can only try. It took a bus ride for Mrs H to discover how much attention Brat Minor devotes to his ablutions. She found herself sitting next to him because her daughter, embarrassed as usual by her mother's presence, had made a point of sitting some distance away. Mrs H glanced at the young gentleman beside her and her eyes focused on his left ear. She was shocked by what she saw. It looked as though some kind of horticultural experiment was being conducted in there.

When I arrived home from work Mrs H greeted me with a vivid description and added, "Go on. Go and ask him what he said when I pointed out the state of his ears." I sought out the little oik and listened to a testimony to the quality of his ear cleaning.

"Do you know," he said with his chest positively swelling with pride, "They say at school I've got the biggest build-up of wax in my ears they've ever seen."

Well, I must say, I would rather my son was remembered at school for his academic successes, the quality of his essays or his mathematical ability. To have people saying, "Do you remember young Haverson? There was a boy whose ears really were clogged up," is hardly something to inspire a family motto.

It was the expression in his voice, exuding achievement, that amused me most. It's amazing how inflexion and tone can enhance the message. He must get this quality from his mother. With adept use of her vast vocal range, Mrs H can add drama, fear and poignancy to the simplest of things.

There's one particular four letter word she uses to great effect. She uses it when she is angry, she uses it when she wants something done and she uses it when she is trying to get round me.

That four letter word is my name. Sometimes, the way she says it makes it sound as though it has more than four letters. And she can deliver it in such a way that it communicates whole sentences.

If I have traipsed through the house with muddy shoes her dulcets pursue me around Fortress H with a "NeYUL!" This says "Oi! How am I supposed to make your children take their shoes off at the back door when their father doesn't?"

There is the blunt version where the "l" is barely sounded. It's almost as if there was a truncated "w" on the end. "Neiw!" This is barked at me when I have dropped my guard and found myself sinking into the sofa. It his her way of saying, "You're not sitting down while I've got all this to do. Kindly present yourself to receive further instructions."

When she kind of yodels my name it generally signals something more to my advantage. Tea is finally ready or she has actually made the coffee for once.

The one to fear is when those four letters are said coldly with the middle part elongated and the tone going quizzically up at the end. "Neeeeyul?" It means something along the lines of "there's lipstick on your collar and it ain't mine".

What I hate most is those odd occasions when she calls me Neily. Yuk! Not only does it make me sound like a professional footballer – Gunny, Flecky to name but two – but it means I am being softened up for something horrible.

I suppose I shouldn't complain. At least then she's being nice to me.

TEENY PROBLEM OF THOSE GROWING PAINS

Fortress Haverson now proudly boasts a teenager among its inmates. This week saw Brat Major cross the threshold and hit the acne trail. Mind you, I'm sure she's been in training for it since she was born. But now it's official. She can be obtuse and sullen and we can say, "Oh well. You know what they're like when they're in their teens."

I still remember vividly the sleepless nights and the nappy changing. A soiled nappy at 4 a.m. for the fifth night running gave me what I believed was a brief flirtation with hell. However, others reassured me by saying, "Don't worry. It's only a 'phase. You wait till they're teenagers. That's the worst."

That comment has come back to haunt me over the last few months as Brat Major's birthday has approached. It's been rather like waiting for an operation. You think the big day is a long way off. Suddenly it's getting nearer and before you know it you're packing your toothbrush to go into hospital and face the agony. But at least with an operation you get an anaesthetic.

Our loveable daughter often plays with some of the younger children who live nearby. She seems to run her own little playgroup. I went to collect her for lunch the other day from a neighbour's house where she had been organising her charges. The grateful mum said, "I think your daughter is brilliant."

"Isn't she just," I replied. From somewhere I summoned as genuine a smile as I could muster to add sincerity to my remark. I did this in the knowledge that within the next thirty seconds this "brilliant" girl would undergo a personality change.

Sure enough, by the time we reached Fortress H the English language had been abandoned in favour of the odd Neanderthal grunt. And as soon as she came in contact with her mother, the sparks flew. A typical skirmish goes like this.

"Your room needs tidying after lunch," says Mrs H. The wordless response consists of inclining the head to the ceiling while executing a theatrical roll of the eyes. This always winds Mrs H up. "Why do you have to be like that?" she demands. This produces what could be misconstrued as an apology. But it's not a straight forward "sorry".

"Sorree!" Heavy emphasis on the last syllable coats the response with petulance.

"If you don't change you attitude you won't go out again this afternoon."

"Yeah, right." Mrs H begins to show signs of leaving the earth's atmosphere.

"Right. You can spend the afternoon in your room." Mrs H will shortly only be visible with the assistance of the Hubble telescope."

"I 'spect I'll live." That bit of lip signals the end of the confrontation. Brat Major finds herself in her room and Mrs H continues in orbit for several more minutes. Brat Minor and I dodge the fall out which will abound until Brat Major has had time to reflect. At that point, Mrs H goes to her room and a frank and open monologue takes place.

From the safety of the hall we can hear Mrs H berating her daughter. The steady drone of her voice is broken only when she ups the tempo to shout "Answer me!" This is followed by a short silence during which, no doubt, the cranial dramatics are being displayed. Mrs H gives up hope of response and resumes her lecture.

The battle ends with a fraught Mrs H steaming downstairs saying, "I've had it with her. You try and talk to her." All this was taking place before she became a teenager. And it's going to get worse? Peer pressure increases as parents let go the reins at different stages and friends find themselves enjoying varying degrees of freedom. One Saturday recently we were in the city on a family shopping trip. In the middle of St Stephens, Brat Major dived into a shop doorway.

"What's up with you?" I enquired when she emerged.

"There's two girls out of year 8 on the other side of the road." She husked. Then added disdainfully, "I can't be seen in the city with my parents. It's so embarrassing."

No doubt the teenage years will have phases of their own. She will probably become a vegetarian, join Green Peace and support the Save the Whale campaign. As she gets older she'll vanish for the summer holidays to work in a bar in Benidorm and announce that she feels a spell on a Kibbutz will be a beautiful and meaningful experience.

Will the day arrive when she turns up at the door accompanied by something hairy sporting an ear ring and ragged jeans to announce she is abandoning our decadent lifestyle to become a New Age Traveller?

Of course, hard on her heels will be Brat Minor and we will have to go through it all again. I don't think I can stand it.

I wonder what life's like on a Kibbutz.

Other books in the EDP Classics series:

NORFOLK – AN ANTHOLOGY
A collection of classic writing from the EDP

FORTRESS H: THE EARLY YEARS

THE TONY HALL CARTOON ANNUAL 1997

TED ELLIS: A TAPESTRY OF NATURE

And also now available:

THE TONY HALL CARTOON ANNUAL 1998

SKIPPER'S BYWAYS
The squit and wisdom of Keith Skipper

NORTH NORFOLK IMAGES

Available at all good bookshops